Robots with AI - will they become like Humans?

Three worlds of different dimensions: calculating, physical bodies, imagination with feelings

Maria Cura

Robots with AI - will they become like Humans?

Three worlds of different dimensions: calculating, physical bodies, imagination with feelings

Bibliografische Information der Deutschen Nationalbibliothek: Die Deutsche Nationalbibliothek verzeichnet diese Publikation in der Deutschen Nationalbibliografie; detaillierte bibliografische Daten sind im Internet über http://dnb.dnb.de abrufbar.

© 2019 Maria Cura
Herstellung und Verlag:
BoD – Books on Demand, Norderstedt

ISBN: 9783738657098

Dedicated to

Paul McCartney

Paul McCartney describes the main aspect of this book with a few words in his song "The Fool on the Hill". Paul McCartney uses art, but in this book it is tried to argue logically and scientific. But logic cannot always express the essence as art can do.

And to Archie Carr and the Sea Turtles

Archie Carr started fighting to protect the highly endangered sea turtles in the midst of the 20th century. As I love sea turtles, I am very grateful to Archie Carr - he began to start conservation programs for sea turtles, when many of them were close to extinction.

From what I am earning of the selling of that book, I will give 1 Euro to a serious sea turtle saving project, because sea turtles are still very much endangered.

Thanks

I thank all my family for being patient with me, if I am again deep concentrated in writing, and then sometimes not having the time for other things.

And I thank the German publishing company BoD.
There I can publish my books without much problems and I can publish them, how I want to do it. I am very happy about that.

Contents

Dedicated to...5

Thanks..6

"The Fool on the Hill" A song text from
Paul McCartney...10

Preface..11

Description of the 4 dimensions: (point), line,
area, space, time..14

Three different worlds - differing into how many
dimensions of the four basic dimensions the worlds
are stretching out themselves.................................28

The amazing working together of the 3-dimensional
physical body world with the 4-dimensional
imagination..33

The difference between the 1-dimensional
mathematical world of numbers and the
3-dimensional physical world of bodies...................39

Having a place..46

Probability...47

What is the difference between calculating the
future or calculating by using past information
and the remembering and imagining of my mind?......52

Is God a huge calculating computer, creating
our world by calculating it?...55

Imagination...59

Along the time-line..61

Time - are there more dimensions of time?................65

The inner free world of the 3-dimensional physical
bodies...68

Counting and calculating need time, and physical
measuring is done by 3-dimensional
objects...76

What change does a higher dimension make:
there are more of open possibilities and the ability
to overview lower dimensions....................................80

What does a lower dimension do to a higher
dimension? It can block the view. It also is
isolating objects by giving them a surface.................83

Measuring and calculating as isolating
process - higher dimensions are unifying and
including inner possibilities...89

The danger of a scientific reduced view onto
the world...94

Robots with AI: deceiving by clever imitation............96

Is energy 4-dimensional, because it needs time
for making a change? Is light close to the mind?......102

Feeling - connected with 4-dimensional
imagination and with remembering...........................104

Will robots with AI be able to have emotions?
And where could be found an emotion-particle,
perhaps in electricity?...108

The togetherness of calculating, mind and feeling....113

Will robots feel emotions like humans? And what,
if not so?...115

Over-viewing events, embedded in great time-
spaces - is this 5-dimensional - when time itself
gets not only a point or a line but a volume?.............117

Epilogue..120

"The Fool on the Hill"

A song text from Paul McCartney

"But the fool on the hill
Sees the sun going down
And the eyes in his head
See the world spinning round."*

The wise "fool on the hill" is not exactly measuring the world, is not calculating hard data, is not analyzing the world around him point after point and systematically. He is looking from the hill onto his wide surrounding with a holistic view, he sees all together as a whole universe, he opens himself towards the width and wideness of time and space.
Is not inside of everyone of us some of the spirit of this fool on the hill?

*Excerpt from the song text of "The Fool on the Hill" from the Beatles 1967 from the album "Magical Mystery Tour"

Preface

There is a huge boundary between calculating computers and imagining and feeling humans: in the way of being and and in the perception. Why? That is what this book is about.

I am not a professional expert in IT or mathematics, but I am interested in these subjects (and other sciences as well) since my youth, that is many years. It may be, that there are important developments I do not know. But on the other side, there is a good chance, that I might see some aspects, that experts do not notice, because I am looking onto these themes more from the outside. Not always it is the only way to understand things from being inside, from being in the middle - it can be that sometimes the view onto something from outside is useful. In German we have a proverb saying: "inside of a forest one cannot see the wood because the trees hinder the view". The experts may judge, if I am able to bring some new interesting aspects into discussion.

AI robots are calculating machines, and for that reason the themes here in this book are circling around the difference of the calculating process and mathematics on one side and the perception of human beings on the other.

The difference is explained with the number of dimensions into which the different worlds of computer and human beings extend. As not every reader may have a clear concept of the four traditional mentioned dimensions (line, area, space, time), there is an explanation of these dimensions in the first chapter.

Computers and robots - even the ones with AI - calculate with mathematical data, with numbers. And these are 1-dimensional. Computers and intelligent robots do the calculation with a hardware, this consists of objects, existing in the 3-dimensional physical body world.

Our human body is also existing in the 3-dimensional physical world of matter and energy. Our human physical body exists for us really only in one moment at once, never at more moments together. And this moment of real existing of our body and all objects around us is moving forward in time. We cannot change this moving in time, we are fixed to this one moving time-point.

But our mind can wander in time: with imagination and remembering. Our mind is thinking and visualizing not in single moments (time-points) but in events, that take time, that last for some time. So our mind moves in a 4-dimensional world. Our feelings are also not point cut, are not only reacting onto the situation in one moment, but are reacting onto greater time realms and developments.

This is a hypothesis. I cannot 100% proof it. So if in future there really should exist robots with emotions and imagination capacity like our human abilities, I will beg pardon from these robots, that I did not see it could be possible. But up to now, from all I know, I cannot believe that robots will become like humans.

I have written already two books in German about the theme with the title: "Künstliche Intelligenz - Werden Roboter mit KI in Zukunft Gefühle haben?" Norderstedt 2018 (Volume 1) and 2019 (Volume 2).
But the theme is not only interesting for German speaking people, that is why I wrote this English summary.

A hint for reading: there is a development in the texts, but the chapters are written that way, that it is most times possible, to read a chapter alone, so that the reader can start at any chapter he likes.

Some aspects will appear more often, because I want to be sure, that I can make clear, what I want to say, and that people coming from very different view-points and background, can understand it.

I feel sorry for not writing in better English, but I cannot afford a professional translator - but I will do my best.

I hope, the text will animate to criticize it, to find own ideas, or wanting to remember something. For that I have left a little open space at the end of every page, so the reader easily can write down his own notes.

Munich in June 2019, Maria Cura

Description of the 4 dimensions: (point), line, area, space, time

This chapter is to some extent the basic of all other chapters in this book. I had written it for the end of the book. It shows the relationship of the different dimensions to each other.

After having written the chapter, I realized that it is so fundamental, that I better begin with it. But nevertheless the following chapters can also be understood without reading this part. For the readers who do not like to read all the here mentioned aspects of the different dimensions, I beforehand mention the most interesting and general aspects of the relations of the dimensions to each other:

A lower dimension confines (and in this way individualizes) parts of the higher dimension.

A higher dimension opens new realms of possibilities. These new realms cannot be seen from the lower dimension, from the lower dimension, the new realms only can be theoretically calculated in an abstract way.

Higher dimensions give an overview over lower dimensions.

Higher dimensions give lower dimensions a place, a location in the wider space.

Here even an speculative aspect is mentioned: A dimension higher than the 4 classical dimensions might be the source for the sensation of the meaning of life, it might be the dimension for the mind behind all that exists. From the highest dimension this mind could be looking with holistic understanding onto all the world. And this mind, overlooking everything (everything that was, that is and that will be), would be able to perceive and understand the meaning of everything.

This chapter is quite abstract (the following ones are less abstract). Here the features of the dimensions in relation to each other are described, they are specified for every single one of the four dimensions.

Traditionally there are known four dimensions: line, area, space and time. By now, in astrophysics some scientists speak of much more dimensions. And also different energies are sometimes named dimensions, mathematics has own dimensions-concepts.

But here the four classical dimensions are meant.

Point:
0 dimensions

The point has no dimension, it has no extension in any direction, it only can be or not be ("Yes" and "No").

From only one existing point, one can see and overview nothing.

Line:
1-dimensional

The line is extending in one direction. It is limited by points: by the point of the beginning and by the point of ending. Positions of points on a line make calculating possible. The points individualize the size of the line, they partition the line, so numbers can be connected with the points on the line. Without limiting the length of a line by defining a beginning point and an ending point, the line would expand unlimited, it would be endless (one exception would be, if the line is forming a circle). The points give a part of line "individuality", give it the attribute of a certain length.

The line can be also divided by points. A line gives the possibility to put points onto a certain location, so addition or subtraction can be done, making the length longer or shorter by adding a part of line or taking it away.

Without lines (or higher dimensional objects), points would not be able to be placed somewhere in a definite way.

The line has no width and no height and no altering in time, it has only a length. Therefor the line is not existing out of physical matter, it has no substance. We would not be able to see a 1-dimensional line in our 3-dimensional world, because of it being without substance. But we symbolize lines for example by drawing "lines" on a sheet of paper. But these "lines" we can only see, because they were printed or drawn with real color, color that is made of 3-dimensional color-molecules.

Lines as symbols are ideal to show the size of a number and to compare the sizes of numbers.

If a man would life in a 1-dimensional world, he only could move along one line (if he has also time, so it is more correct to say, he would life within two dimensions, line and time, because without the dimension of time he could not move at all - but here is meant 1 dimension of the room).

In a 1-dimensional world one can look at points on the line, but at no points beside the line. If the points are transparent, one can overlook all the points on a line. If a point is not transparent, one only can look until to this point, but not behind it. For looking behind it, one would need a higher dimension.

If a line is very narrowly curved, it begins looking more like an 2-dimensional area, but it still remains a 1-dimensional line. And a person, that would live in the 1-dimensional world, would not be able to realize the curves of the line, for him the line would be straight, because he would need the understanding of a second dimension to recognize the curves.

Area:
2-dimensional

The area is extending in length and in width.

An area gets both limited by lines and divided by lines (lines that are straight or curved). Without these lines areas would expand endlessly (the exception would only be an flat area where the ends are meeting like in a ring). Limiting lines give areas "individuality".

Without areas (or higher dimensional objects), lines would not be able to be placed somewhere on a definite place.

The area has no height and no altering in time and therefore also cannot exist as matter, it also has no substance. In our mind can exist areas, for example the area of a football pitch, or the area (plot) that is bought for building a house. But in the real world these areas are not really without height, they only are thought without height. In reality for example there are small stones and plants on it, so the area would never be really flat. A picture is nearly an area, but being existing of molecules, it is not really flat. But in mind we can imagine areas that have no height and are timeless. And mathematics can calculate areas.

Areas are the surfaces of our 3-dimensional world. These areas are normally not flat, they have an irregular surface - but this surface is on the topmost surface nevertheless without substance (what you see is the matter beginning at the surface) - otherwise it would itself be an 3-dimensional object with an outer surface. This 2-dimensional surfaces are limiting 3-dimensional objects. Without surface-areas around them, objects would not end, they would expand into the space. So the surface of our body is isolating our body from the surrounding, the circles of an elementary particle of an atom forms a surface around the atom, this "surface" one could say, separates the inside, where the atom begins and the outside, where there is no atom any more.

If a man would life in a 2-dimensional world, he could recognize lines and points, but he would be unable to realize any height, it is a total flat world he would live in. Even if the surface would be not flat, the man could not cross the space outside his area. He is fixed to the 2-dimensional area, he perhaps not even would realize, that the surface is not flat.

From an area one can look at lines on the area. If the lines are transparent, one can see all the lines on an area. If a line is not transparent and so long, one cannot go around it, one can only look up to this line, but not behind it. For looking behind it, one would need a higher dimension.

If an area is crumpled and curved, it begins to look more like a 3-dimensional space, but it still remains 2-dimensional, if seen as a surface.

Space:
3-dimensional

The space is extending in length and in width and in height.

Space is limited by areas, these areas are seen from us as surfaces. Without limiting surfaces, the space (or objects within the space) would expand endlessly (an exception is a curved space, as our universe might perhaps be).

Without space, it would not be possible to place areas (surfaces) in an definite, unique and individual way at a certain location.

The space alone has no time, cannot change without time. Therefore it also cannot really exist without time in our changing world we live in. The space needs at least a now-time-moment moving on the time-line to be existing in our world. But we can think a pure space, because in mind it needs not to exist in time, we can imagine an unchanging space without time and the pure space can be calculated by mathematics.

If a man would live in 3-dimensional world without any time moving forwards, he would see no changes at all, all would be unmovable.

From a space one can look at areas in the space. If the areas are transparent, one can overview all the areas in a space. If an area is not transparent, one can only look up to this area, but not behind it. For looking behind it, one would need a higher dimension. This can be the time with it's possibility to alter things.

When a space is showed at different time-points (as in a film with 24 or more pictures in a second), it looks like existing in a continuous time. But in reality there are only many timeless not moving pictures (isolated time-points), simulating a moving time.

Time added to space:
from 3-dimensional to 4-dimensional

That is the world we really physically life in. Objects there have length, width, height and they exist in a time, that is passing by - so they age and change.

But the existing is fixed to a single moment, it is this moment that is moving through time along a time-line. It is the moment, that gives space a place within the time.

But the moment itself is without duration, it has no time-length, it is like a point without any dimension (extension). So one could say, the "now-point-moment" (as it is here called) is not making the world 4-dimensional, the world remains physically 3-dimensional, fixed to the "now-point-moment". Time begins to become a dimension when a stretch of time is looked over in its length. An event, lasting over the stretch of some time is 4-dimensional.

Without the changing of space (or the objects, that need space), it would not be detectable, that time moves on (for measuring time, we need watches with moving watch-hands or other moving elements inside). Now-moments without changes then would seem endless. The changing of the 3-dimensional world makes time-moments individual, makes it possible to distinguish the moments.

Time-points (with the "now-moments" of ending and beginning) limit the endless row of changing, they make it possible to distinguish and to individualize single events.

Time makes it possible that things can change (in some way the 3 dimensions length, width and height could be seen as changes in location in space as well, changing takes place in the "coordinates". That is a mathematically look on to it, but for not abstract thinking humans, this is not the same as changes in time).

An event is existing of 3-space-dimensions and of a stretch on the time-line (from the beginning point moment of an event towards its end point moment). The time (as 4th dimension) with space is the basic that our changing world can exist. And our 4-dimensional mind is necessary to realize and understand this world with its continuous events.

Is our world forming and created within the mind? That is what Buddhists say. In monotheistic religions, the world was formed by the mind of God - so even here is the idea to be found, that mind is the source of being. Or was always everything together: mind, time and 3-dimensional physical world? Or is mind evolved out of time and physical world? Perhaps we can never solve these questions scientifically.

Our mind can jump over the strict time-line, it can look ahead in time: it can imagine the future or it can look back: memories. So the mind is much different to our 3-dimensional physical world that is fixed onto the "now-point-moment". We can understand events as changes that take time, we can see changes from the beginning to the end as an whole event. This is the theme of this book, and the question, if robots with AI are able to do the same. The first spontaneous answer might be: "yes, they can, they can calculate events". But is that the same as our mind sees and understands events?

Lower and higher dimensions

As the lower dimensions are limiting the higher dimensions, it is only logical that by calculating on the 1-dimensional level it is possible to find out, what will work in the physical world and what is physically impossible. This also is true for the 3-dimensional world, because even the 3-dimensional world is physically limited by linear sizes.

But feelings and meaning of life are open to wider realms, they have a connection to the whole, their sources are not only the limited objects, their sources come from the open wideness of space and time. And coming from there they are combined with local and time-wise limited objects and events.

A higher dimension opens new realms of possibilities. In our life it is possible with our mind to understand objects and events as a whole, and to perceive them together with emotions. The new realms of a new dimension cannot be seen from the lower dimension, the new realms only can be theoretically calculated in an abstract way - that is what calculating AI computers and robots are doing.

It is most unlikely to understand mind, emotions and the meaning of life by looking only at limited dimensions. Even more unlikely it is to understand mind and feelings in a deeper way, if one tries to use only 1-dimensional calculation. 1-dimensional calculation can tell if some preconditions for physical developments are realistic or not. But they cannot tell, if these developments make really happy or give a feeling of being connected with the meaning of life.

It is our mind, that perceives the 3-dimensional physical identifiable objects as objects. It is the mind, that sees a table as a furniture, on which one can put plates and meal or a computer. Under the pure physical aspect, there are only certain wood-molecules stuck together, and at the surface of the outer wood-molecules there are flying around the gas molecules of the air. But even the molecules are only energy and small elementary particles, that without a mind looking on them have no name and are not belonging together in a deeper sense, they are only being hold together by energies.

And it is our mind, that is perceiving connected events within the time. We can see a tennis match as one whole event. In the world without mind, there are only energies influencing matter.

The mind has a wanting, it wants to do something, to achieve something, and under that requirement it is seeing objects and events.

A computer or robot with AI, can it perceive objects or events as well? I doubt, that it does it in the same way as our mind does it, but I cannot prove it. At least there has to be the first initiation given from a human programmer, a programmer, who has an aim. He will be the first "teacher" (programmer) for the AI robot, he will teach it to see whole objects and events and to evaluate them in their function. So there is some initial part within the computer program, that comes from the human mind. And perceiving objects and events by calculating does not mean, that there are feelings and emotions connected with the result. Valuation yes ("it works" or "it does not work"), valuation that is connected with the result - but feeling and emotions?

A 5th dimension?

A higher dimension makes it possible to overview and understand the lower dimensions from a higher level.
And a higher dimension gives the lower one a location, a place.

Aims give objects and events a place in our live, they make objects and events either important and wanted or feared or uninteresting. And the sentiment, when they are close to the meaning of life, gives our aims the position, the place in our life.

Where does meaning of life come from?

It might be possible, that there is even a higher, perhaps a 5th dimension, from where the sentiment of the meaning of life comes from. I am not talking about the mathematical or astrophysical higher calculated dimensions, from these I do know too little.

If our mind for example is able to overview events and aims in an holistic way, it might be, that this happens out from a higher dimension viewpoint. Perhaps basic emotions and the sense for the meaning of life are at home in this higher dimension. This higher dimension would allow to understand better the basic connections, the meaning, that for us lies behind everything, because it allows a wide view.

It may be, that meditation as well as praying, that ecstasies in shamanic rites and that also real love could be means to get into contact with the higher dimension. Or these opening practices are already part of a higher dimension.

If this is so, then it is easier to understand, that the contents of religions and spiritual ways are not oriented on physical and calculated facts. Then it is not primarily important, that these facts are scientific true. Then it would be the main aim of religious and spiritual practice and tradition to open the mind for the higher dimension. Perhaps this dimension is the mind behind all of what is existing. From the highest dimension this mind could be looking with holistic understanding onto all the world. And this mind, over-viewing everything (everything that was, that is and that will be), would be able to perceive and understand the meaning of everything. To get into connection with this mind could then be very wholesome for us.

Building higher dimensions takes time - a highly speculative picture

If a point is gliding along a line (like a pen), it is building this line and needs time for it. If a line is gliding along a surface, it "experiences" the surface and by that is needing time. If a surface or an area is gliding through a space, it is experiencing space during the time. If space or an 3-dimensional physical object is existing along a time-line, an event is created. If all events ever are taken together, they are becoming the whole world in its eternal dimension. Do we as humans have to live for a certain time with different events and a mind perceiving these events emotionally, to enter by this way with theses experiences into the space of eternity? This will remain an open question, as long as we are bound with our lives on to a dimension lower than eternity.

Three different worlds - differing into how many dimensions of the four basic dimensions the worlds are stretching out themselves

We can experience at least three different worlds: first: the abstract mathematical world of quantities that also use robots with AI, second the world of physical bodies, and third the world of imagination, memories and feelings.
These three worlds differ in the amount of dimensions into which they stretch out into.

The abstract mathematical world deals with quantities that can be expressed by length. Every number can be shown in a line of a certain length, can be compared this way or connected with other lines (numbers). So the mathematical world is 1-dimensional. Even if we describe a cube, which is 3-dimensional, we do it by multiplying 1-dimensional numbers (multiplying is a special way of adding - and gaining the result can therefore be symbolized by stretches added one after the other in a single and 1-dimensional line). Only the physical unit that is written behind the number, tells us, how this number is related to the more-dimensional physical world - but the calculating itself could be done without physical units as well.

The world in which our physical body is existing is 3-dimensional. It needs space to exist, it extension stretches in all space directions (length, width, height). But it is existing - as we see and experience it physically - always only at one point of the time. The time in which physical bodies are in our world is only a point of time. This 0-dimensional point ("now-moment") is wandering ahead in time. But we cannot physically go backwards or forwards from this now-moment, we are connected with this point in the line of time. We are physically existing from one moment to the next moment. We are not existing at two moments together or even more and we cannot jump physically quicker forwards or instead backwards in time.

But our imagination, our remembering and our feelings can overview a development within time. We can imagine something happening, can imagine it from the beginning to the end and every other moment-point on the time scale. So our mind is capable of perceiving connected developments, our mind imagines a happening as something that happens in space and during some time. So our mind is capable to comprehend a 4-dimensional world.

Our imagination might not always fit into the physical world - then we can feel it, if we try to live after the pictures of our imagination. If we close our eyes and walk ahead because we imagine, that ahead before us there is free space, then we will hurt ourselves, if over there really in that moment in the 3-dimensional world there is a wall standing in the way. Our 3-dimensional body will collide with the wall and we will open our eyes to control our picture that was only imagination.

But in other cases, our imagination can lead to plans and changing the 3-dimensional world in an effective way.

Imagination is free to change things. In my imagination, I can put away the wall. In what cases this is useful, that is another question. Maybe a town-planner will tear away the wall in his imagination and then in his planning, to get a new passage. So imagination is often having an effect on the 3-dimensional world when it leads to actions within the 3-dimensional world. But the 3-dimensional world on the other hand can correct physic or other incorrect imaginations (for example psychological misunderstanding - so can I get a slap in the face, if I say something insulting), and we learn this way more about the 3-dimensional physical world, and what is possible within it and what is impossible.

But bumping into a wall is a process that can as well be described with 1-dimensional mathematics. I can calculate the place where the wall physically is standing, and I can measure my distance and can then calculate, when by moving with a certain velocity I will touch the wall. This is a certain moment, one point on the time-scale. I can also calculate different moments and see, how far I am from the wall at many moments.

The bumping into a wall can be described by many many single points - but it is a 1-dimensional description, on the basic of single points. One can connect these points to a curve - but one can never be hundred percent secure, that between the calculated points not something extraordinary will happen (for example, if a meteor falls down on the wall, or a friend is calling me from behind). In mathematics, if there is no external happening that must be thought of, one can be sure. But in the complex 3-dimensional physical world, there only exists a relative security.

The calculating 1-dimensional world is never the same as the real physical 3-dimensional world. And when a computer or robot is steering an 3-dimensional physical object, it has to be done by a 3-dimensional physical hardware computer or robot and the process of calculating itself has to happen with something real physical, in the computer it is a current flowing. If an intelligent computer program is constructing a 3-D-object, the calculated object needs to be constructed by a physical 3-dimensional apparatus with a physical 3-dimensional material. Even if pictures and videos are shown on a screen, directed by a calculating programmed computer with AI, the particles or the light waves building the picture on the screen must exist in the real 3-dimensional physical world.

The 1-dimensional calculation world can have calculated influences in the physical 3-dimensional world - but pure mathematics (not the physical electrons working in the computer) is never the same as the physical 3-dimensional world. It may be a basic to the 3-dimensional world - but it is not the 3-dimensional world itself. That is a great difference!

A physical 3-dimensional object does exist without calculating. It is just there in all its size and power. If not so, every-thing would have to conduct huge calculating operations at every moment: the particles of an atom as well as whole gal-axies and the streams of light. But they all can follow the mathematical natural laws without any computer - at least no one up to now has for example seen an intelligent computer existing in an electron. This is miraculous to us, we cannot tell, how the 3-dimensional physical world is fulfilling the mathematical laws of nature.

But also the 3-dimensional physical world of bodies is not the same as the 4-dimensional mind.

The amazing working together of the 3-dimensional physical body world with the 4-dimensional imagination

I think, most people - like it was with me before as well - are not astonished, that our physical body exists for us only in one moment at one time, at the "now-point-moment". And that this "now-point" glides constantly forward on the time-scale from past over present towards the future. And all physical things around us do the same, they share the "now-point-moment" with our body (not hundred percent exactly, as Einstein has taught us, but in our personal life this effect of relativity does not show itself in a way, that we can sense it). Our table does not run quicker through the time, or the chair, or our friends, do not grow older much slower than we. That is the reason, why we can measure time with the help of watches and have a constant, reliable result on this way.

Is this not astonishing and fascinating, if we think of it? Many astonishing things we do not realize, because they are so common for us, that we do not think about it, that it could be much different.

With our physical body we cannot leave the "now-point-moment", our body is fixed to it. We cannot wander backwards in time with our body nor forwards into the future. We cannot make time pass slower or quicker, we have no might, no potency and no simple knowledge (Einstein´s relativity theory is here again an exception) to manipulate the time-flow.

I think, our body is in view of the time without stretched time-dimension, it is existing in a "now-point-moment" without further extension, the "now-point-moment" has no stretch, it is over in the next moment, you cannot realize it without it being already over. It resembles a point in space, that has no length, no width and no height.

So pure physical bodies cannot compare a situation in the past with the situation in a next moment - because this would need to stretch the time to be able to make an comparison. When I walk three steps, then to be able to tell that I have walked three steps, I need to compare the starting point with the present point - and that means looking into the past.

A pure physical body without mind - as far as we know - cannot look into the past or into the future, it is just existing as it is in the "now-point-moment" (but the body´s situation in the now-point-moment was created by the past, but that does not mean, that comparing the now-situation with the past is possible).

Measurement and recording and even the then following calculations are only understood in their meaning within the passing time, when the results are interpreted by a mind, that has an understanding for at least for the 1-dimensional passing of time, a mind that has a concept for the phenomenons of past and future.

Does that mean, an intelligent computer has an understanding concept of past and future and passing time? No, it only calculates mechanically and can decide that something is correct or not correct ("Yes" and "No"). But that is not an "understanding", only a following of rules. Time is in calculation only another thing to describe with 1-dimensional numbers. The whole calculation a computer makes, where there time is involved, could as well be made without "knowing" that it is a calculating with a factor of time. The physical unit tells the computer how to operate with the numbers (adding, subtracting, multiplying, dividing and all operations derived from these). But even if the computer (with AI or without) is capable to get results, that fit to the outer world and that can regulate physical bodies in a positive way - that does not mean, that even an computer with Artificial Intelligence has an lively understanding of passing time. The time-factor is only a calculation-operation-rule.

But the mind of living beings can understand the fading time to some degree (but time always remains a little bit mysterious). We know, that there are moments that lay in the past, and we are expecting the moments of the future. It is the human mind, that has watched the passing time and has begun to construct clocks and to find mathematical formulas to calculate with time, with the intention to be able to say more about the running time and the happenings within the time. But a pure physical body without mind, would have perhaps been able to build something, that measures time (for example a natural build sun-clock), but it would be by accident (for example this might be a way in which evolution made more precise time-feeling possible within living beings). But the human being knew consciously about the passing time and invented clocks with the aim (and not only accidentally) of measuring time.

This is possible, because the human mind can remember the past and imagine the future. The human mind (and most probably also the mind of animals, perhaps to some extend also plants) can understand stretches of time as something whole, he can see an event as a whole happening. He does not only see fixed, stiff, isolated situations appearing one after the other, each one for itself. He sees what is happening as a continuous time-stretch. For the mind to look on the world it is necessary to add the time to the perception of space (and the recognizing of 3-dimensional bodies within space), so the mind sees the world 4-dimensional. Time is not seen only as a "now-point-moment", but it is seen as a stretch from beginning to end of an event (or some part of the happening). Our mind does not look on the world like a camera, it does not produce single snapshots, but it is more like a video. The mind is more like a video we see (with pictures too quick following each other as that we would realize the single pictures) or an imagined story in a book, because the mind can run forward or backwards in time, can stop at some situations or jump over a part of time. Or the mind can ignore some situations and wander further into future.

So I can remember my holiday, I can look on pleasant happenings more closely and I can leave out boring times. I know, the boring times were there as well, but it is not interesting to look onto them closer. Or I can plan my holiday, and in my imagination I see events, of which I hope they will come true, I can play with them in my mind, to see, how it would feel for me. I will not imagine unimportant things, but I will more clearly try to imagine the highlights of a possible holiday. And perhaps I will connect memories from a former holiday at the same place with the coming holiday: "perhaps we will meet again this nice family and then we can…"

And "having experience" often does mean, that in the past I have tried out something in the real world, in the 3-dimensional world and I have learned, if it did work or not. For us the 3- and the 4-dimensional world are interacting permanently.

For me it is very astounding, that a 3-dimensional body can have a 4-dimensional mind working inside.

If my memory of the past is becoming false, this could lead to not welcome situations. A simple example: if I think, that I remember quite well, how I cooked a special meal, but in my memories one important ingredient is forgotten or remembered wrong, then the meal will not taste very well.

Or if my imagination for the future is wrong, and I want to make something come true in the 3-dimensional physical body-world, then I will learn, that this is not possible and my imagination, that it would work, is an illusion.

My life consists of both: on one side there is my physical body existing 3-dimensional at the "now-point-moment" and on the other side there is my 4-dimensional mind, remembering past and imagining future and trying to let the positive imagined situations become real in the physical 3-dimensional world (or to avoid negative imagined situations).

There is a permanent interaction of physical body and mind. And this makes living very interesting and variable. It is like a permanent game: imagining something and finding out, how to make it come true in the physical body-world. This physical world is on one side existing only in the "now-point-moment", but it has the power, to correct our imagination. So in one way the mind with its imagination has power over the 3-dimensional physical body-world, but also this world has correcting power over the 4-dimensional mind world.

I only can say, this is fascinating me. It is so normal to us, that we normally do not think about it - but if one begins to look on it, it is very amazing.

The difference between the 1-dimensional mathematical world of numbers and the 3-dimensional physical world of bodies

Mathematics is operating with numbers. A number is 1-dimensional, every number can be expressed by the length of a line (the length between two points, which are the beginning and the end of the line).

And every calculation, how complex it might be, is consisting of these 1-dimensional numbers and the result is again a one-dimensional number, that can be symbolized by the length of a line. One could imagine the whole calculating operation as an operation, in which a line of a certain length gets diminished and or extended one time or many times after special rules. But all that can happen in the 1-dimensional world alone, without other dimensions.

And if one is calculating a figure with different angles, and this figure is therefore 2- or 3-dimensional? Then the angle can be expressed by a 1-dimensional number (and this number can say something about the length of two 1-dimensional lines in a triangle for example).

Everything from our physical body world needs to be reduced into 1-dimensional numbers, if it should become a part of a mathematical calculation. What cannot be 1-dimensional counted, that cannot be calculated. So emotions can only be part of a calculation, if the emotion is put into a number. That happens, when people give "likes" with a click in Internet for news or videos. Then the "likes" can be counted easily. Or another trick is, that a product in a shop can be valued by a number up to 5 points. Then the computer can count the points and calculate an average valuation.

Measuring for calculating means cutting down and breaking down the 3-dimensional world into 1-dimensional numbers.

The world can be described in mathematical terms - but only in a limited way from the outside or with the measuring or calculating of special points. But the whole inner meaning we can feel, can not be described by mathematical operations.

To make adding or diminishing in a calculation correctly corresponding to our world, there have been found formulas. By the way: to find formulas, something must be able to be repeated many times. But what is, if there are things, that happen only once or very seldom or not regularly? It may be, because there is a chaotic background, or we do know up to now nothing scientifically about such happenings - but does it mean, that then they are impossible - I think not. Formulas do guarantee (normally) that the result will be in the right relationship with some physical value in the 3-dimensional world. To make it identifiable, which physical sizes (measured sizes of the 3-dimensional world, expressed with a 1-dimensional number) go into a formula, the numbers get physical units like "km", "kg", "hour", "velocity" and so on. But nevertheless the numbers remain numbers, and one can calculate the same thing also without physical units, the result in numbers would be the same - one only would not know to what physical body unit this result would fit.

But the result is a 1-dimensional number (to which is added an physical unit to understand to where it is belonging in the 3-dimensional world). The result is never the 3-dimensional physical world itself. The result only symbolizes an analogy to the 3-dimensional world. That is also the reason, why a number can be attributed to everything. The number three for example can be attributed to apples (it then describes the number of apples), to kilometer, to ideas, to a chance to win, to minutes, to possible variations, to probability and so on. The number itself remains "untouched" by the unit that is written behind the number.

The 1-dimensional (symbolized in a straight line) offers possibilities in one direction only. There can be infinite lot of numbers on a line that are greater or smaller than one special number (for example there are infinite many numbers smaller than 2 and infinite many numbers bigger than 2. Even if it is a line for example limited between the numbers 0 and 3, there are infinite possible numbers, as the place behind the decimal point can be extended endlessly. But if one takes an 2-dimensional object (not a line, but an area like for example a rectangle), the possibilities are even more: infinite multiplied by infinite. This is, because besides the infinite number of points on one line, there is added an infinite number of possible lines. In the rectangle they can lay one beside the other. And because a pure line has no width, into a rectangle (or into any other area) fits an infinite number of lines. And if one takes an 3-dimensional object, there can be infinite 2-dimensional areas within the 3-dimensional object. And if time is added, the possibilities are even more, because in every moment the 3-dimensional object is no more exactly the same as a moment before, because the 3-dimensional object is aging. And perhaps the object itself or its surrounding is changing by aging.

Each dimension is adding more possibilities.

So in mathematics theoretically situations in many dimensions can be calculated with the right formula. But nevertheless the used numbers and the number-size of the result are 1-dimensional. Mathematics can calculate more dimensions, but the calculation itself remains always in the 1-dimensional world. One cannot touch or smell or hear the pure number (for example the number 5), it has no substance itself.

The higher-dimensional worlds have an inner aspect, that is no more calculable for the 1-dimensional mathematics. Mathematics uses values that describe limits, the numbers describe the beginning (starting-point), that is the number zero, and the end-point, that is telling the number, at which length the line would end, or where a room ends, or a situation is ended, or something is full, or something would change, and so on. The end-point of a number (its value) is always talking about the point, where something ends, something is limited. But a number never tells something of the situation in between. It is like the length of a way described as airline-distance or linear distance. But in reality, if a car drives this distance, it is a much longer way with a lot of curves. And for an crawling insect like an ant, it would even be much more longer, because it would have to crawl upside and down over every little stone. And a molecule would have to crawl inside every very small scar on a stone and out again. So the pure straight length between two points does not tell the whole reality.

In the 1-dimensional world, a line (symbolizing a number) is understood as to be straight. But is it really so? In the real more-dimensional world, the line could curve, it could swell, it could go through other times (perhaps in parallel worlds). So there could happen things, we do not know about, when we only look on the 1-dimensional world of calculating and mathematics.

And even, if everything that we calculate, "runs straight", it is not possible to calculate everything, just because of the immense number of influences physical objects are exposed to.

If we would try to calculate the future movement of every water-molecule within the ocean, we soon would see, that this is impossible. A water-molecule of the ocean is influenced by neighbor-molecules, these themselves are pushed around by their neighbor-molecules. The different temperature in different regions is playing a role, the wind, the rain, earthquakes, lava coming up in the ocean, the inside heat of our earth, sunshine and clouds, animals and plants within the ocean, human activities, chemical reactions in the ocean, changing gravitation by moon, sun and galaxy...

I cannot imagine an intelligent computer, that is able to put all these things in the calculations of each single water-molecule. I cannot imagine, how much Artificial Intelligence it would need. And then there as well are many chaotic systems in this oceanic world. These chaotic systems are not accurate calculable. They bring numbers in the formula, whose numbers in the places behind the comma are not ending. That has the effect, that by summing up all the minimal differences behind the comma, it might come to chaotic reactions, that might have a big influence, but could not be calculated before.

But the ocean does exist. It is a real 3-dimensional object. It has inner qualities, that cannot get perfect and wholly calculated. It can be measured (also only approximately) from outside, but its inner situation is no more describable, if one tries to be complete. Of course, special factors can be calculated. Calculating is good in isolating phenomena or by calculating the probability of future happenings of bigger units. But calculating is not able to describe the whole of 3-dimensional physical objects in every aspect. There is an inner abundance in the 3-dimensional real world, that never can be totally calculated.

But nevertheless: the 3-dimensional physical body world exists. And is it imaginable, that the atoms for example, always calculate their position and all the influences, that are having an effect on them? I can imagine better, that the 3-dimensional physical world is just existing by itself, following the nature laws without calculating them, by "knowing" how to "behave", just by it being, what it is. But perhaps this question, if nature is calculating, will never be answered.

Having a place

Real 3-dimensional physical objects have a certain place in a space of unknown width (universe) and in time of unknown length (perhaps eternity). And in this realm, whose limits are unknown to us, they are in relation to all the surroundings.

Calculation only can create relation with given data, each relationship has to be programmed. Reality is just as it is, and it is in relationship to all other physical objects.

Calculated "virtual objects" have no personal space and they have no personal time in the universe, no space or time that is reaching out over the small calculated realm, they are calculated in an anonymous realm, and they can be used for different objects. For example, the static of a house, calculated by an architect with a computer-program, this static is fitting for every house of the same type. While calculating, only the given data are put into relation to one another, but the calculated virtual object can be used where ever it is fitting - or also not at all.

Real 3-dimensional objects have a real place in our world, they are individualistic, they exist only once. Objects with the same shape, function and so on may exist more often, but each of these objects has its only single place in space and time. Objects are singular in the 3-dimensional world of bodies. They can change and they do change, but the substance and the energy of them do not get lost, they remain somewhere in the universe.

Probability

With the help of probability we can calculate things that for some reason are impossible to be calculated individually. With probability they can nevertheless be calculated approximately.

In calculating probability a group of events - often out of the total group of events - is taken and it is registered how many elements go this way and how many another way. It can be calculated from the percentage, how the total group will most probably split into the different ways. Or it can be told by probability in percentage which way future events will show up and turn out. In this probability-calculation it is assumed, that the percentage in the observed smaller or in a similar or in a past group is the same as the percentage in the total group or in a similar one or in a future group. Examples for this are: a survey before an election, or the radioactive decay, weather forecasts.

But also our mind permanently uses probability for decisions. If I have more often bought apples in a shop, where many of them were too old and had putrid spots, then I will expect that to happen the next time as well (high probability seen from my former experience) and I will decide to go to another shop, even if that shop is more expensive or farther away.

Some things are just easier to calculate with a smaller group and probability, but a lot of things cannot be exactly calculated, and probability-calculation is the only way, for example: the moment when a single radioactive atom will decay, or the place of an electron circling around a nucleus. But in finding out the probability, forecasts for greater groups can be quite reliable.

But probability cannot end into a clear statements for a single individual. It only can say what is more probable. When in a country the forecast says 60 percent of all people will vote for a conservative party in the next elections, then the probability that I will vote for this party as well is also 60 percent. But that does not say very much, if I personally really will vote like this. I perhaps might vote for a party that is almost unknown and has only 0,5 percentage probability to be voted for.

Probability is looking from a distance (onto a group, not a single person) and is enlarging this group, saying, that all of the total group will behave like the little group (or a similar or a later group). The individual is not interesting very much.

By looking on a greater group, probability-calculation is like a simulated higher dimension, it seems like looking from a hill over the land. You cannot see every single detail, but you get an overview. But in reality even in the overview the details (unseen) are existing (if I am standing on a high hill, I cannot see every plant, every insect, every molecule - but they are there), in the probability-calculation the details of the whole are nowhere. That is because no data of every single object are given, only an data-excerpt.

Calculating probability can be very useful (for example for planning the density of public transport). But it can as well be a little bit strange, if the results are attributed to single individuals. Recently I read a headline: "Every person produces 85 kg garbage" (in a year). It is meant, on an average every person produces 85 kg waste - but to say (as it does the headline, with believing that everybody knows how it is meant correctly), that every person produces 85 kg is nonsense: it would imply that you and I and my neighbor and my colleague, everyone of us would produce 85 kg garbage, not more and not less.

This example shows, that probability is not apt to describe individual situations. And where there it is only possible to calculate probability, the calculating computer or robot is blind for the individual situation.

A shop-trading company can, when it is observing and registering my clicks, tell that I would perhaps buy a certain article, because many people that made the same or similar clicks as I, bought this article. But if I really will buy that article, an online-shop computer even with the best algorithms and high Artificial Intelligence cannot know.

Maybe there is also in many systems (not only in the mind of humans) a freedom to decide, that makes secure prognosis impossible. This is perhaps the case in situations, where chaos plays a part. But it is difficult to say, if it is real freedom. It may be, that we only do not understand the influences, that lead to a certain decision.

But interesting is, that time is a factor, that in passing by, is converting probability into secure individualistic ways, ways which then really have been walked.

In another picture you can say: if the now-point-moment passes over a situation, the openness of the situation with certain probabilities is changed into a defined situation, in which each individual (men or atoms or whatever) has its clear place, its clear choice. In the future there is probability and open possibilities, in the now-point-moment the situation changes, probability is changed into certainty (which can differ for an individual from the expected probability) and individual decision. In the past things have happened and cannot be changed any more (at least in our world).

In pure calculating this is not the case. You can calculate the same thing again and again, without ending. You can calculate $63+29=92$ a hundred and one times - it will always happen to have the same result. There is no changing probability. But you can change parameter as you like, you can calculate $63+29-3+3=92$ and so on, and you can return again to calculating $63+29=92$ - it makes no difference to the result, and the result does not show, on which way it became that number (only added units might give a hint - but even units don´t tell anything about the way of measuring, how and where and when measuring was done).

In our 3-dimensional world everything from the elementary particle to a galaxy is unique and individualistic.

In a purely calculated virtual world, there needs to be artificial individualization, because numbers only are individual in respect of their position to other numbers and their relation to the other numbers (an example of an characteristic of a number: a number can be divided by another number, without remaining something left). But there is no individuality for numbers within the 3-dimensional space or time. But objects in the real 3-dimensional world have an individual place in space and time and in so many relationships to what is around them. Numbers are only in some way individualistic in a 1-dimensional world.

In calculating, a place and a time can be given artificially. Then the number is described as a number symbolizing a time or a place in space. But nevertheless the numbers are only numbers. But a computer can direct things in the 3-dimensional world - for example the pixels of a picture on my computer screen or on a robot screen. Numbers only can give these pixels of light a real place and a real time of happening, because the shining of the pixel light happens in the 3-dimensional world (and has therefore a real place and a real time of existing in our world). And the regulating, the steering, is also managed by electrons and computer and robot hardware that are also 3-dimensional in our physical world of bodies.

Our 3-dimensional world is an individualistic one.

What is the difference between calculating the future or calculating by using past information and the remembering and imagining of my mind?

One difference between calculations and the mind working, is, that the mind deals with facts connected with things that happened in the 3-dimensional world. Or the mind imagines things, that might happen in the future of the 3-dimensional world.

The calculation deals with 1-dimensional numbers. These numbers may be symbols for really measured facts. But inside the computer- or robot-program they are 1-dimensional. They can be changed in every way by the person or by the apparatus that enters the data.

The "data" our mind is working with can be changed by fantasy, but the remembered data are not totally free selectable, they are connected with the 3-dimensional world. Our memory might be not hundred percent correct, but it can not freely choose. For example: if I have never been to the moon, I cannot have a real memory of being on the moon. A computer program, if it has enough data, can always simulate an object being on the moon, can calculate the influence of gravitation on that object, the influence of heat and cold and so on.

But the result of a calculation depends on the data measured and entered to the program. The memory that is in the mind depends on experience with the 3-dimensional world, a world that is connected over many influences from one end of the universe to the other. Nothing there happens totally independent. The calculations in a computer - even in a computer with AI - are isolated and only describing a sector of the 3-dimensional world. There can be even entered absolute nonsense-data into a computer-program, chosen by a random generator - and the program will calculate them. Mind can invent many new and even absurd things, but there will always be some psychological reasons, why a mind is imagining things in a special way. The mind is not bound to the now-point-moment, but it is nevertheless always connected to the 3-dimensional world and to all the influences of this world, that reach the mind. And for example, to see simply a cup standing on a table, is a result of many uncountable factors of our 3-dimensional world.

Calculations run 1-dimensional, but the mind overviews the 3-dimensional world as it is unfolding in time, so the mind has the capacity to see things from a higher level. Calculations simulate a 3-dimensional or even with events a 4-dimensional world (or mathematically even much higher dimensions), but they construct it point by point, and by connecting these points in a straight line. The mind looks on an event from above, looks at the whole as something that belongs together. The mind does not see in points and lines, but it realizes a whole picture.

And an important difference to calculations is, that the mind connects the data with feelings, with emotions. Feelings judge - not in the simple way: is functioning or is not working ("yes" and "no" of a calculating program), but in the way that something is giving joy and happiness or contentedness or not. The single emotion is connected in the background with a feeling of meaning, that in its last end is no more describable, but nevertheless it is essential to the mind.

Is God a huge calculating computer, creating our world by calculating it?

Are we and our world created by a big calculator? When we see, how modern computer games can create worlds, then, on the first look, it is not so absurd to think, that our world we live in, was also created by a big computer with AI and is run by it.

But the simulated computer worlds are relatively small in comparison with the real 3-dimensional world we live in. The computer world has a select number of conditions, in our real world everything is influencing everything and that on many levels. And also the illusion to observe an almost real world in a computer-simulation is to a great degree owed to the ability of our mind: when our mind is seeing simple lights popping up at certain points on a screen, the mind is combining these lights in a way, that they seem to be objects and persons. It is the ability of the programmer and later of the Artificial Intelligence, to arrange the lights on the screen in a way, that our mind thinks it is recognizing things in a world.. But the house, the person, the reasonable action of the game is generated in our mind with our imagination. The computer has only received data and has calculated them like the program is demanding it.

But it seems, that the computer knows and understands, what we humans want to see. But it does not know it in an under-standing way, it is only fulfilling of programmed tasks, and is, when the computer has Artificial Intelligence, learning as the program demands it. It looks like the computer seems to know, how it has to change the outlook of the screen, so we humans could think, that there inside the screen is a real man running or a bird flying and so on. But there is no real man running on the screen.

A real man, that is living in our world, is under all the influences of the real physical 3-dimensional world. Only a few of the conditions that influence a human being are programmed in a computer game, even if it would be a computer with AI. Programmed may be perhaps how arms and legs move or how a face can change the expression. It might be, that the effect of gravitation on that simulated body is programmed (so the person can simulate jumping) - but if I begin to lift and shake my computer or my robot, then it will have no effect on the simulated computer-person - there only would be an effect, if the computer or robot would end working because of the shaking (but that would be anyway the end of the game).

A computer or a robot with AI that is calculating, needs hardware, which is only existing in the 3-dimensional physical world. So if our world would be only a virtual world, than behind this virtual world nevertheless a 3-dimensional physical world with time passing by must exist. Or if that world would also be a calculated program, then behind that world again a 3-dimensional physical world would have to exist. Or behind that world, if that would be also an calculating program. And so on.

It is like in a hall of mirrors: dozens of mirrors reflect me and my world - but all the reflections come from flat mirrors, even if they give the illusion of a real and 3-dimensional world within the mirror. But somewhere in the hall of mirrors there must be a real 3-dimensional physical world, otherwise there would be nothing to mirror. If I am not real as a 3-dimensional physical body within the hall of mirrors, I cannot be reflected from any mirror. The amount of mirrors can be risen, but there for seeing something must always be a real 3-dimensional world with its objects inside the hall of mirrors.

So the idea of the world being created by a godlike calculator does not really help to understand creation. It still would be a miracle, why there is something - even if we would think, that worlds could be created by computer programs with Artificial Intelligence.

In the bible it says about creation:
Both citations from the: English Standard Version (link: https://www.bibleserver.com/text/ESV/Genesis1):

1. Mose 1:

1 In the beginning, God created the heavens and the earth.
2 The earth was without form and void, and darkness was over the face of the deep. And the Spirit of God was hovering over the face of the waters.
3 And God said: "Let there be light," and there was light.
4 And God saw that the light was good. And God separated

the light from the darkness.

5 God called the light Day, and the darkness he called Night. And there was evening and there was morning, the first day.

6 And God said, "Let there be an expanse in the midst of the waters, and let separate the waters from the waters."

Joh 1,1:

1 In the beginning was the Word, and the Word was with God, and the Word was God.

2 He was in the beginning with God.

3 All things were made through him, and without him was not any thing made that was made.

4 In him was life, and the life was the light of men.

So the bible looks on creation to be a work of the mind, of the mind of God.

The people, who believe, that we are created by an intelligent artificial computer program, believe that a world can come up by 1-dimensional calculations.

Buddhism does not say anything about the beginning of the world. But the 3-dimensional physical world of bodies is for Buddhists only an illusion of the mind. Behind that illusion there is the real nature of mind or of spirit.

To me it seems, that scientifically it is not possible to tell, where our world comes from. Science can look on lower dimensions than the dimensions our mind is living in. But it cannot see, where our mind is coming from, and to what our mind is linked in its deepest meaning.

Imagination

Amazing: in our world 3-dimensional physical bodies exist all together at one time point (now-point-moment). Perhaps there might exist other worlds with other time points running in another way (for example faster or slower or jumping or changing forwards and backwards) - but if so, we don´t know about it.

The mind is other, it can move freely in the realm of time, overlooking whole time-spaces, wandering forward or backward, combining experiences of the past with expectations of the future, changing things in imagination.

Is imagination calculating single time points of a situation and connecting them (like in mathematics, where two points of a curve are connected in a straight line)? Or is imagination working different, is it looking onto a whole event from above, that means, not looking on single time points, but on the whole development as one whole happening. It means, seeing the event gliding incessantly through the time, and not to imagine an event as doing hopping from one calculated time point to the next time point.

A physical body in our 3-dimensional physical world is a whole thing (with all its inner world) and it is like this without calculation. And just like that, most probably the imagination of an event is an imagination of something whole, and not of something being detailed calculated. An event is looked upon as something that is seen continuous as a change within the passing time.

This is a theory. If this theory ever can be proved scientifi- cally, I don´t know. But I also think, it cannot easily be dis- proved.

Imagination and remembering are looking from above on to lower dimension-levels, and in this way remembering and imagination are having an overview, an overview over the space of time of an event, and they see an event not in sepa- rated points but as something complete.

Along the time-line

There is (from our point of view and in our experience) a straight time-line, along which the now-point-moment is moving from the past over the present moment towards the future.

Turning around and walking back into the past is not possible for our 3-dimensional bodies, we are fixed to the now-point-moment, together with everything surrounding us.

The past no more can change (from our point of view). Our memories can change a bit (or sometimes a lot), but they cannot alter freely, we cannot change them just as we like. If we are creating a new situation of the past in our mind, it is no more pure memory, but our mind is using fantasy to try to find out, how the things could have developed other - perhaps to change behavior in the future.

So the past can no more be altered on the 3-dimensional physical level, and normally it alters only a bit in our memories.

This absolute stiff character of the past regarding the 3-dimensional world is essential to our world existing. If the past could change, nothing would be solid, everything would waver. One moment the world would be like this and in the next moment it would be much other - because everything that changes is influencing at the same moment a lot of its surrounding (if not even all of the surrounding). And the past is so long a time, so that there would permanently be changes (at this or that point of the past) that would change everything in our present. So nothing would be reliable, perhaps it would not even be possible to recognize anything, because things would not exist long enough in the same way to learn recognizing things. In such a variable world no continuous development, like it is normal in our world, would be possible.

Our world has developed on a stable basis, on a past that does not change any more. The situation at the now-point-moment is granted to be as it is. This situation has emerged from the past, and only if the past is fixed and alters no more, one can rely on it and build the future world from it.

The changing of the real 3-dimensional world is happening exactly at the now-point-moment. That is the moment, that is flexible enough to change things (with the help of energy). But this moment is also standing at the edge to become a past moment within the next moment. And in this changing of one present moment becoming a past moment, the things get fixed. And not only one change gets fixed for ever as an past change, but uncountable changes all over the world and together with that all the influences the changes had in that moment on their surrounding.

So the past is stable and fixed, the now-point-moment is open for changes, based on the situation the past has created up to that moment, and the future is even wider open. The future contains uncountable possibilities, of how the 3-dimensional world could develop. The preconditions, that means the world as it already is (as it has developed in the past) are limiting to some extent the open possibilities of the future, the possibilities, that can be realized, that can come real. But still there is a vast openness of possible developments. The further away in future, the more possibilities open - it is alike the light of a candle, the candle light is spreading far out into the room, the greater the distance is, the wider the light is spreading. But the further away in future a single possibility is, the more unlikely it will come true, because many changes before could go another way (it is as it is with the candle-light: the more it is spreading into the room, the more dim it will become).

A development needs time (needs the now-point-moment, that is going along a certain stretch of the time-line), so a development is 4-dimensional.

Developments - both possible ones and impossible ones - can be imagined with the mind.

In the virtual world the situation is other. Even there logically one thing has to happen behind the other (so in a formula for example it is clear, if first the summation or the division has to be calculated). But sequences can be repeated, can be altered, can be deleted. In the 3-dimensional world this is not possible for past events.

Also in a film for example scenes can be cut out or added, they can be modified, put at another place and so on. In many computer games the player has the possibility to start again either from the beginning or from a certain point of the game.

A video film even can be run backwards, what to us seems very funny, for example, if people all are moving backwards or a stone is jumping out of the water.

An IT-programmer can alter the program, so that the conditions for a special situation are different, and the input of data has other consequences than before.

But the world in a film or in a game is very small in comparison to the universe and an alternation may not have so much consequences. And also even an intelligent computer program with AI only deals with some aspects of our world. But if the computer program is beginning to regulate things in the 3-dimensional real world, then it really might have sometimes a greater effect on the 3-dimensional body world, if the programming is changed.

Worlds can be very different in respect of the dimensions. And as the influence of the 1-dimensional calculating world is nowadays growing rapidly, we have to realize more clearly and try to understand, what it does mean, what effects it has on our 3-dimensional physical world and on our mind.

The working together of the dimensions in our world nevertheless is quite amazing and wonderful.

Time - are there more dimensions of time?

Time is for us in some way 1-dimensional - it moves on along one line from one time point to the next, forming this way a straight time-line beginning in the past, reaching over the now-point-moment into the future.

But what would it be, if for us time would be higher-dimensional? Would it be possible to go "sideways" - like a point on a 1-dimensional line that only can go following the line, but on a surface with width and length, the point can go sideways, and in a space with a height it could even rise or sink.

What could it mean, if we would have more time-dimensions, beside our now-point-moment line? What could it mean to "move sideways" in the time? Could it be, that there are parallel universes, in which parallel time-lines (time-strings?) are existing? Could it mean, that all the possibilities that are open, are existing in parallel universes, where other decisions as in our world are made? This was already discussed in connection with the (thought-) experiment of Schrödinger´s cat, which at the same time might be alive and dead, until someone is looking at it (who wants to know more about this quantum physics thought experiment will certainly discover enough in Internet).

Changing is always combined with time. In our world there only is possible one change at one time-moment - and it remains the only change of something at that now-moment for the rest of the time-line. But if there would be 2-dimensional time, in which more time-lines would have place (like lines on a flat 2-dimensional area), if one could go sideways within time, there perhaps could be more simultaneous possible changes at the now-point-moment, so for example in the thought-experiment of Schrödinger´s cat, the cat could be on one time-line alive and on another dead.

And if the time itself even would be 3-dimensional? Perhaps then the laws of nature would not be any more a limit to changes, all would be possible. Perhaps this would be the emptiness of the Buddhism, where everything is no more separated and nothing is isolated, no body thing, that can die or disappear is there - perhaps everything is and is not at the same time. But this is a very very speculative thought.

One other very speculative thought I had when long ago I was writing my book "Möglichkeitenraum":

Perhaps is every concentrating or compacting movement a time that moves backwards into the past. And also the energies like gravitation or powers that are holding together the particles of an atom, would belong to the time moving backwards. And every extending or exploding movement (or energy) is time moving forwards into the future. And appropriate to this theory, we would be living in a world with a certain mixture of time-backwards and time-forwards. If this mixture remains stable, all that are living in this world with this certain mixture could realize the same things around them, because they all have the same time-velocity. Perhaps this time-velocity is given by our mind, and beside this time-velocity many other time-velocities are existing, but we cannot perceive them.

Is our mind able to wander in higher time-dimensions? I am not sure. But our mind can imagine different scenes, in our fantasy we can play a situation in different ways. A football-fan for example could remind himself of the yesterday game and before his eyes he could see what would have happened, if for example the goal-keeper not would have been able to catch the ball, or if the referee not would have given the red card. An author can write down the end of a story, but later on might change it. So our mind can imagine different changes in a certain situation, and in some way so it is building in fantasy different time-lines - is this a 2-dimensional time? And how could be a 3-dimensional time in our mind? Is it that what Buddhists call "Enlightenment", is it, when we feel the presence of God and of eternity, both being timeless? Is it a feeling of being one with everything and everybody? This is a question that perhaps never will be answered.

The inner free world of the 3-dimensional physical bodies

With the inner free world of the 3-dimensional bodies here is meant the possible variations an unit can have, without loosing the character of that unit. For example: a human can be great or small, can be European, Asian, Red Indian or African, he can have blond or dark hair, he can speak English or Japanese, he can have blue or brown eyes, be left- or right-handed, he can be conservative or progressive, female or male, old or young - but he or she is always human, belongs to the unit "human", to the human race.

Ahead of calculating it is necessary to do isolating and making definitions of borders (beginning and ending). It has to be defined, what is characterizing a certain type and what is another type. But the inner zone between the borders of beginning and ending (ending = the points, where something is beginning to miss the characteristics of its type) is left open. The inner zone is the realm, where the characteristics of the type get fulfilled - with only one possibility or many. That could even be a simple 1-dimensional line of a certain length, but then not many variations are possible (only dividing the line with points), there is only existing a single dimension of possibilities. That is much different to the above mentioned type "human", where there are very many variations possible in the inner zone.

But all real 3-dimensional objects have an inner realm (containing one or infinite many possibilities), even then, when this zone should be empty. It then is a realm of open opportunities and it is possible to fill something into it, therefor it can be called a zone or space for open possibilities.

But all real 3-dimensional objects have an inner realm (contain one or infinite many possibilities), even then, when this zone should be empty. It then is a realm of open opportunities and it is possible to fill something into it, therefor it can be called a zone or space for open possibilities.

The inner possibilities of a 3-dimensional physical body are calculable only if there are clear conditions and a small amount of possibilities, and there are no unknown curves and bendings between the two points of a measurement for a calculation.

But most 3-dimensional physical bodies contain unknown inner possibilities and these a computer, even a computer with AI, cannot calculate.

A measured value that results in a number, is only correct, if the line between the beginning value and the ending value is straight. If there are unknown bendings and curves between the beginning and the ending point (or other anomalies, depending on what was measured), the calculation becomes wrong. This would for example be the case, if in greater distances, like to a satellite, the relativity theory would not be included into the calculations. But we cannot always know or predict all the factors, that might make a curve in the line of a measuring. For example, in the calculation of social development many factors may lead to curves within the calculated development, factors that were not foreseen before.

But the real 3- and 4-dimensional world contains from itself (without doing calculating) all curves and bendings, and contains as well all possibilities in the space, the realized ones, and the open ones.

It is difficult to calculate even such a seemingly simply thing as the length of a coastline. How subtle a distinction is one going to make? There are bendings of 10 km or of 10 meters at the coastline - at what degree they will still be measured and considered? Or the bending, that a rock makes at the coastline, should it be considered? Or the bended surface of molecules? The result will differ dramatically, depending how exactly and detailed I will measure the coastline. This is something the chaos theory has demonstrated.

To calculate the sizes and all the possibilities (the realized and the not realized ones, which are many many more) which our whole universe is containing - I think the calculator that is able to do this, that perhaps must be even more huge than the universe itself. But if the number of possibilities is infinite, they never can be totally calculated.

To calculate, what really has been realized, would be an immense task. But to calculate everything that has up to now not been realized, but is in the realms of possibilities (that means, it could once in future perhaps be realized) - that seems even more impossible.

But nevertheless, our world contains all these innumerable open possibilities. To some extent, we can feel the open realm of possibilities (without calculating): an empty room has more open possibilities to be furnished with furniture of a new person, that in future time will be living there, than a room that is already furnished. And we feel the freedom, to be more free with furnishing in the open room, while a dense furnished flat gives us another impression.

The computer or the robot only can calculate how big in cubic meters a room is, but it has no feeling towards the result. It can learn, that more open cubic meters means more open possibilities. But the computer cannot calculate all single open possibilities, and it has no feeling of "free space" as a human being would have. The open space in a calculation of a computer is no real extension of a real room, it is only the calculation with the help of limit-points. But our feelings in our mind can feel the real extension.

Let me try to explain the problem in calculating the inner world of 3-dimensional physical bodies in another way.

The inside of 3-dimensional physical objects seems to be not totally calculable.

For example, I will here again describe (as already further above) the ocean. The ocean is the greater unit. The inner free world of this unit are all the permanent changes an ocean is showing and nevertheless still remaining an ocean.

It would be a problem to calculate exactly and detailed the physical object of an ocean on earth, for example with all the total of its water molecules. Each one of these molecules is moving every moment in a partly chaotic way, and alone from that chaotic way, its movement is already not hundred percent predictable.

Each molecule is influenced by the neighbor molecule and these neighbors are themselves also influenced by their neighbors - so all the molecules of the ocean are in a way influencing each other.

And there is also an influence by the temperature, the weather with wind or storm, rain or snow, but also through the gravitation of the earth, the moon, the sun and the galaxy. Earthquakes and lava, water-streams like the golf stream, live within the sea like fish and plankton or whales, men and ships, all the other non-water molecules, chemical reactions, exchange with the air of the atmosphere - it all will influence the water-molecules.

To calculate all these factors for the future movement and exact position for only one water molecule seems impossible (besides of the problem to get the totality of the necessary data). Even farther away from being possible it would be to calculate the future movements for the totality of all molecules in the sea (the same it would be for all molecules in the air).

The same it is for the snowfall. One can speak of the unit "snowfall", for example the snowfall at a certain day in a certain region. The inner free world of the unit snowfall are the possibilities, how many snowflakes will fall down and which way they are taking during falling down. It could perhaps be easy to simulate snowfall by randomly showing snowflakes on a screen. But in reality, besides of chaotic incalculable influences, there are many small but calculable influences on each single snowflake. There could be the wind, even a very very light one, the temperature, the consistency of the snowflakes, the way how each single snowflake is constructed (no snowflake is exactly like the other, they are all different in the form of their crystals). But all these influences are having an combined impact on the snowflake in the real world. They cannot be ignored, if a world like the real world should be constructed within a computer. It is not so difficult to calculate a great amount of snow. In this way, it might be estimated in a weather forecast, how much snow will fall in a certain region. But to calculate the real way, which each snowflake will take, when it is falling down - that seems impossible. The realm of inner possibilities (all the different ways down the snowflake could take when falling down) that is open for each snow flake (combined influences then let the snowflake take a definite way) seems too huge for calculating.

A third example of a realm of great inner possibilities of variation: A tree species with its characteristic leaves. A tree of some sort has typical leaves, it is a general characteristic appearance, that each leaf of a type of tree shows. But each leaf is a little bit different. If objects are industrially produced by humans, one of these objects of one sort looks like the other of the same sort. But in nature, there are types, and they have in each individual always a new varied form. Nature is able to vary the type a million and more times, without falling out of the limits of the type. There within one sort of trees, there is an abundance of possible variations of leafforms. It may be, that each leaf of one tree species, that has ever grown over thousands of years on millions and millions of trees, nevertheless was unique in its form. There is a huge inner variety-freedom within the form-type of leaves from a special sort of tree. Could we calculate, how a leaf on a certain tree on a certain branch will exactly develop? What different influences do have a modifying power onto the growing leaf to give it an individual single shape?

These almost unpredictable situations exist not only in the vast ocean or in the air or in plants and animals and humans, but also in most of the existing things.

But even, if it would be possible, to calculate all this - to me it seems, that it would need a gigantic calculator, an enormous computer with AI. And this computer has to be built from 3-dimensional physical bodies, and run by energy moving inside of that 3-dimensional computer or robot.

Instead of total exactness often probability is better to calculate.

But nevertheless our world exists, and in the moment (the "now-point" on our time-line on which we are moving forward), we look at something that has come true in an individualistic way, everything has a decided position. In experiments of the quantum physics this decided situation seems only to arise with the watching of the process by someone. And in quantum physics the question has come up: is the world only decided in that moment (now-moment), when we look on it? That would mean - in view of the here explained hypothesis - that the 3-dimensional world only gets really decided and fixed in the "now-moment", when our 4-dimensional mind looks on it (is it then necessary, that the mind is recognizing what it sees, or is it enough, to see without recognizing?). But this is a new theme, and that is too big for me.

Counting and calculating need time, and physical measuring is done by 3-dimensional objects

Before calculating, counting is necessary. And counting is always taking time. For counting you have to look first on one of the objects, that have to be counted. This object has to be isolated in perception from the surrounding and from the other objects. Then you (or the computer or the robot with AI) will look onto the next object and find out, if this object belongs to the category of the objects to count. If it is so, "2" can be counted. And so on. But this isolating one object after the other needs time - however little time it might be, it is time.

In counting, an information won a moment before ("there is one object of the wanted category") is added to an information that gets won a moment later ("there is second object"). Without looking back in time to the former won information, counting is not possible. Even if counting is only done with pure numbers and without any further objects, counting takes time, because the person counting (or the computer), has to remember which number came before to know which number comes next.

So without time no counting and no calculating is possible. Quite practically we realize that, when our computer or a robot needs some time to do an operation.

For measuring (which is a special way of counting) as well as for calculating, an 3-dimensional object is necessary: either a human being or a technical object. If not a human is measuring by experience or in other ways, then an apparatus is needed, that measures. Measuring things in the 3-dimensional world cannot be done by virtual means alone. Objects can be calculated, after some data have been measured: for example one can calculate the volume of a cube, if before the calculating the length of the sides has been measured.

So for every calculating of things in our 3-dimensional world by the computer, there before was an 3-dimensional apparatus necessary for measuring the needed data. And the computer or robot itself is 3-dimensional. And the human or even the intelligent computer needs a little bit of time, to do the calculations.

So in the end, it is perhaps surprising: the calculating of a virtual looking back in time or of a view forward in the time, mathematical calculating of that, what had happened or what will happen, even this virtual calculating of time-sequences needs 4 dimensions: 3 for the measuring apparatus and 1 more (time) for the calculation process.

Was the 4-dimensional imagination, was the 4-dimensional mind of living beings necessary to "invent" counting, mathematics and calculating?

If - as some begin to believe - we also only live in a gigantic computer with Artificial Intelligence, if our world only would be calculated with mathematical processes - where then are the calculations done? Is there a 3-dimensional material calculating our world? Is for example inside of an atom getting some calculation done? Or is outside of our view existing a gigantic 3-dimensional super intelligent computer, doing all this calculation? I do not really believe it.

And as measuring and calculating needs 3-dimensional physical apparatuses, it is more the other way round (not the real world needs a calculating, but the calculating needs the real world to make an real effect): if the virtual computer world has to create something new in our world, it needs either the 3-dimensional physical world (for example a 3D-printer with real material to print), or it needs the 4-dimensional world of our imagination. For example: a video film is physically only existing in isolated light-spots popping up at different screen-points, moment after moment. It is our mind, which is putting together the light-spots in a way, that a scene of our 3-dimensional physical world is simulated in our mind.

An AI computer can learn to describe this scene as well with attributes, but it was a human mind first, that developed a program for the AI computer, so it is now able to learn. And the computer is learning how to differentiate things, but in a black and white view: "yes it is an object, a reaction, a scene like this or it is not alike". The AI computer does not learn to feel emotions by looking on the screen. It only can judge corresponding to a given aim. The AI computer is deciding in a factual way "positive in respect of the aim or negative".

Without the 3-dimensional body world, there would be no computer, no robots, no Artificial Intelligence, there would exist no computer programs calculating, but also no human brain.

What change does a higher dimension make: there are more of open possibilities and the ability to overview lower dimensions

What happens, if to existing dimensions a new dimension is added?

One aspect is, that the amount of open possibilities is increased.

Most probably the increasing of possibilities is limitless, because on a 1-dimensional line, there are infinite many points. On a 2-dimensional flat surface, there can lay infinite many lines with infinite many points. In a 3-dimensional space, there is place for infinite many flat surfaces with infinite many lines with infinite many points. In a 4-dimensional time combined with 3-dimensional space, there are infinite many time-points where a space is existing with infinite many flat surfaces with infinite many lines with infinite many points existing for the now-point-moment.

Each point on a line, on a flat surface, in a space and at a time-point is an individual possibility. This point - or the line, the space, the moment, can be part of a thing: for example the point of an atom or molecule, of a chair, or the point of a part of the foot of a human - that means that this point of the foot is existing in a special point of the space and at a special time-point.

So adding an dimension is increasing the amount of possibilities enormously.

But there is another effect that comes with a higher dimension: from a higher dimension one can look down on lower dimensions and one can have an overview.

If you only have 1 dimension, the line, you can only look along the total line, if there is nothing nontransparent between you and the end. If there is something nontransparent in the way, you only can look until to that point and not further.

But if you are on a 2-dimensional flat surface and there is a small point blocking your way of sight, you can at least look in other directions, or you can stand sideways and look on the line with its point from the side. Then you can see, at what position the point on the line is laying, and how long the line going on after this point, and if there are more points on the line behind. But from a 2-dimensional position, you cannot look behind an opaque line (a 1-dimensional object) that is running over the total surface, the long line does not allow you to view onto the other side, lying behind the line.

If you are living in a 3-dimensional world and you have the possibility to rise, than you can overview a 2-dimensional flat surface, and you can see all the points and lines on it. That is why a map or the photographs of Google Earth are taken from a position high above the land (satellite). Standing on a mountain you can overlook the land down below.

But if you live during a time-space, if you are in a world, where the things can change within time, you can look onto a changing 3-dimensional space. You can overview events, from the beginning to the end.

So generally an object of one lower dimension can block the overview of parts of the dimension you yourself are living in. But if you are rising one dimension higher, you can overview the dimension that was partly hidden for you before.

And higher dimensions give lower dimensions a place: the point has its place on the line, the line in the area (surface), the area has its place within the space, the space is existing in the now-moment, and the moment within the event.

Generally the higher dimensions give more space for possibilities, for more freedom of choosing and for more overviewing. And they offer place for lower dimensions.

What does a lower dimension do to a higher dimension? It can block the view. It also is isolating objects by giving them a surface.

An object of lower dimension can hinder the sight in a higher dimension: the point can block the free sight onto the total length of a 1-dimensional line. A line from end to end can hinder the sight onto the total extension of a 2-dimensional surface, a surface can block the sight of 3-dimensional space (a curtain - 3-dimensional but in its function near to 2-dimensional objects - for example hinders to look out of a window), and a 3-dimensional unchanging object can block the development of events that are 4-dimensional.

An object is cut out of the vast infinity by the surface of an lower dimension. For example one cannot look through the surface of an in-transparent object into its inside. And a hard surface hinders an impact, so the impact is not fully reaching the inside of the object.

A 1-dimensional line is ended by point (without dimension).
A 2-dimensional flat surface is cut out into a special form by a 1-dimensional line (for example cutting out a square or a circle with a line). Borders of a country are 1-dimensional lines (the country then is looked onto as a 2-dimensional flat surface).
A 3-dimensional space or body is divided by 2-dimensional surfaces: the skin is limiting our human body, the wall is the

border of a house, the circle of the outer elementary particle of an atom is the border between atom and the surrounding of the atom. Of course a skin or a wall have a thickness and are in this way 3-dimensional. But the surface of the skin (not the skin in its full thickness) is the real border between man and surrounding. And the surface of a wall of a house is the limiting of the object "house".

A 4-dimensional event, taking time, is limited by its beginning and its ending - and these are situations in a 3-dimensional space (or even less dimensions), they are not 4-dimensional. Situations as the beginning and as the end are not changing in themselves, they are only single moments, points on the time-line so they remain 3-dimensional, while the whole event is a changing situation and by this is 4-dimensional. Begin and ending are like the surface for the space - they are cutting out an event from the endless eternity.

The limiting of the higher dimension by a lower dimension is resulting in cutting out objects or events. It is a process of isolating and individualizing.

For recognizing something, for communicating and as well for calculating it is necessary to isolate objects by making definitions of borders: something is that, if... or if not.... This means defining something, and in the realm of dimensions, this is done by the next lower dimension.

The inner realm of the higher dimension is left open by the limiting lower dimension. But all objects have an inner realm, even then, when this realm should be empty. It then is a realm of open opportunities, you can fill it with something or you can call it just a "space for open possibilities".

(I have written a book in German about the space of open possibilities. It is called "Möglichkeitenraum - Die unsichtbare Fülle des leeren Raums" in English I would translate the title: "The Space for open Possibilities - The invisible Abundance of the empty Space" - but I have not yet translated it into English.)

In general and also in our 3-dimensional world the inner realm, never can be the same as the calculated outer borders. Our real world is existing with the calculable borders but also together with the not calculable inner realm.

An object, calculated by the computer, is never identical with an real object with inner realm. A 3-D printer can calculate the surface of an object and then print in 3-D. But the inner realm of this 3-D object is not an inner realm produced by the calculations, but an inner realm being constructed by a 3-dimensional printer with 3-dimensional material.

A robot that is smiling, is making the gesture of smiling by imitating in a calculated way the outer surface of the form of smiling. But this has nothing to do with inner feelings.

Making something alike in respect of the outer form is quickly giving the illusion that the objects are really alike: it looks like the original is the same as the constructed. But in the inner realm they need not to be alike, most probably they will not be alike inside.

Because calculated in a very advanced way, the illusions of robots and products being constructed by computers with AI, will be more and more deceiving. From the outside they will look more and more like natural and even living products. It will be necessary to get a more precise knowledge, a knowledge what the differences between original and imitation are. There are new questions arising.

The lower dimension is limiting. The natural laws in our 3-dimensional world are limiting the possibilities in our world as well. They decide, what is possible for a physical body. Are the natural laws a dimension as well? This question I leave open here.

Our mind is able to ignore natural laws to some extent - not totally, because our fantasy is also influenced by our experiences in the 3-dimensional physical world. We can imagine for example, to beam us from one planet to another, as in the series star trek. But if we try to make our fantasies come true in the 3-dimensional physical world, we will learn, if the fantasies are conform with the natural laws, or if they are contradicting them (or if we just do not yet know enough about the natural laws and how to use them). If I try to run through a wall, I will feel painfully that this is not possible for me in my physical 3-dimensional surrounding.

This limiting and correcting is a way of interchange between the 3-dimensional physical world of bodies and the 4-dimensional world of ideas.

I add here a short excursus of another observation: to some extent, gravitation makes us humans (and animals and all objects on earth) to partly 2-dimensional bodies: we mostly walk on the surface of the earth, we cannot fly without technique, we can only jump, to leave the earth surface for a short moment (and even in an airplane we must have contact with the bottom of the plane). Our surface has to have contact to the surface of the earth, by standing (with the feet), sitting or lying. It is contact from surface to surface, not from inner substance with inner substance, we are not mingling our body with the physical body of the earth, we are only touching its surface with our surface, the border between our body and the earth surface remains. But in swimming and diving we can use the space in its deepness, the surface of the water-molecules around us is holding us. I have realized that in observing sea turtles: in the water they are swimming easily and seem weightless, but on land, when they are crawling on the sand of the beach to lay their eggs, they seem to be almost heavy as a stone, .

In working with our hands, we do use the 3-dimensional space (but the hands are connected to the arms that hold them in contact with the whole body, that is connected with the earth-surface). As far as our body can reach out, in this surrounding we can use the 3-dimensional space, but for reaching higher, we need a ladder, that is offering a higher earth-surface-platform. So we are 3-dimensional physical bodies, but the effect of gravitation makes us being also bound to the 2-dimensional surface of the earth. But without the gravitation of the earth, for example as astronauts, humans and objects can move freely in the 3-dimensional space - but the astronaut and the objects around the astronaut loose their solid ground, that is holding them in position on earth - the live is not getting easier.

Walking on earth, we are to some extent bound 2-dimensional, from the effect of gravitation. But this is true as well for a ball, rolling on the surface. Has gravitation something to do with limiting and compressing the dimensions? Another open question. At least the gravitation of the earth is saving us from going lost in space. And the gravitation of the sun is binding the earth so it gets not lost in the vast and cold cosmos, and the center of the Milky Way does the same in respect of our galaxy.

Measuring and calculating as isolating process - higher dimensions are unifying and including inner possibilities

To measure something, it first needs to be isolated from the surrounding.

I now say some things about calculating. As I have not studied mathematics, I am not absolutely sure, if what I am saying is always true, or whether there are mathematical situations, where my observation is not valid. But as I think for a lot of mathematical situations, what I am saying is true, I will continue:

What has diffuse borders, is not beginning and ending clearly and by that cannot be measured exactly. In that case a decision must be made, at what point one is putting the beginning and the ending. In calculating there is no fluent change, there has to be decided "yes" or "no": yes, there still is, what has to be measured, or no, there it is no more. Or the change has to be described by an exact beginning and an exact ending size within that range it has to be calculated. But there is no diffuse open range in calculation.

Even if probabilities have to be calculated, there has to be a clear number, expressed in percent, or there has to be a definite range with a certain beginning and a certain end, for example: "for 22 to 31 percent of the people it is expected to vote for the left wing". The sentence "quite some people will vote for the progressive party, but it will not be a majority" may be interesting if you are listening to the news. But it is impossible to make a useful calculation from this sentence. The utmost you could say mathematically from this remark is: people voting for the progressive party are less than 50 % but within more than 1 %.

If it is defined, what an object of counting, measuring and calculating is, and what not, then one can begin to look (in a definite surrounding - not in the whole universe) how many objects with the alike quality characteristics can be found. Then they can be counted, every object must be isolated in mind (or from the computer program) from the next one, and to each one only one time gets attributed a number. If all isolated alike objects have a number (and the numbers follow the scale one after the other, without leaving a number out or using one number two times, beginning with 1), then the highest of the numbers tells, how many isolated objects there are.

And if I also have other objects, which have been isolated for identification and have been counted with its own series of numbers, I can calculate for example: if I have the number of kilometers walked and I know the time I had needed for it, then I can calculate my average velocity by dividing the number of kilometers through the number of hours (but I cannot calculate my velocity for every moment).

What are kilometers in that case: isolated stretches, one after the other, the next kilometer always beginning where the previous kilometer is ending. The counting of the length of one single kilometer is beginning with zero meter and ending with 1.000 meter - then the new kilometer starts. That is quite commonly known, but nevertheless it is interesting to look at it, because, we make it normally automatically.

It is similar with the time. On a analog watch the time is made visible through the movement of the different watch-hands in a circle. Each circle is either a second, a minute or a an hour. So by this trick, the time is made visible in another dimension. It is now possible to express the length of a time-sequence with the length of a distance, it is the stretch of way that a watch-hand has moved itself forward. Time in this way becomes a 1-dimensional line, and can be now calculated.

But, as we see, it is essential not to count double or leaving something out. And in counting distances it is important to count one element of an unit following exactly after the other, and not leaving empty spaces (of distances or time) in between. So you have to know exactly, where something, you want to count, is beginning and where it is ending, and also that there is no uncounted interval in between.

Measuring and counting needs exactly isolated things. As measuring, counting and calculating are operations on a ba-sically 1-dimensional level, it is normal, that things have to be isolated and have to be measured and described in the be-ginning in 1-dimensional facts, so you get 1-dimensional data. This is like a skeleton of the world, but there is missing the flesh.

Looking onto the world from a higher dimension, the look becomes unifying. Things that are contained in a higher dimension can be seen in its surrounding, without measuring and describing 1-dimensional attributes as length, height, width, weight, temperature, velocity and so on. You can realize all these attributes at once, when you are looking on something from a higher dimension: the weight and temperature you can feel, the size you can see - you can realize them all at the same moment, because they are there altogether in the same moment. You see a tree, and you don´t divide it into its length, its height and width to have an impression of its size. You see a curve, and you don´t have to measure it in one-dimensional data to know if it is an narrow curve.

The question is, if our mind is working with the basis of 1-dimensional data and if it is changing these data by calculating into more complex information. But however it is, in the end we have an impression that is holistic.

And by looking on objects, we get a not calculated impression of inner possibilities. So if we see an empty room within a flat, we feel that there are many possibilities to furnish it - much more possibilities as when the room would have already partly be furnished. We see a ball and know it can roll on the ground. Maybe this is experience, but maybe we also have a deeper understanding for the possibilities of objects, than calculation based on 1-dimensional data could give.

And we can look on whole scenes from above without analyzing details. So we can enjoy the wide view from a high mountain. There something inside us is feeling the vastness of the land, is opening the heart towards it. Our mind can open towards infinity and eternity.

The danger of a scientific reduced view onto the world

Some sciences give the impression that data won with eye, ear and nerves are put into a calculation program in our head that is alike to that computers or robots work with data. Perhaps this is really a part of our cognition - but if our cognition is more than that, if there is an mathematical incalculable part of our realization, what is then? Then the observing and measuring in the 3-dimensional world cannot detect the real volume and essence of the 4-dimensional world our mind lives in. The mathematical world only can calculate the world with the help of 1-dimensional data. So calculation can find limits and changing points, but it cannot describe all that is happening in our 4-dimensional mind.

To prove the above statement is also almost impossible, because the proof would need a scientific description of the 4-dimensional perception. But that would be as if a blind person should describe colors. But if a blind man would say, colors don´t exist because he cannot see them, that would be foolish. So the hypothesis, that the mind perceives the world partly other than science can describe it, should not be be denied for the only reason because the science up to now has not proved that the mind is working different. When science cannot prove the other functioning of mind, it does not mean, it is not like that, it only means, we do not know for sure.

The 4-dimensional world most probably will not contradict the natural laws found within the 3-dimensional physical body world. It is just another level, being combined with the 3-dimensional world. For example: when mankind learned to speak, that changed the world by giving the possibility to write down and copy experiences and much more. It accelerated the development of culture. But it did not change the natural laws of the 3-dimensional world - it only added something to it, that before was not there. So the 4-dimensional world is adding something to our world, that in the pure 3-dimensional world is not existing.

But if it is demanded, that there is no other world than the 3-dimensional physical world of bodies, then that could reduce the look onto the world and onto the world our mind can perceive. Decisions made from this smaller worldview might be bad for the freedom of mind and for a deeper experience of the world.

Robots with AI: deceiving by clever imitation

In older times there was believed, what in German is called "Signaturenlehre" (doctrine of signatures). It means for example, that something that appears similar to a part of our body, might be a good medicine for this part of the body. For example red things could be a good medicine for the blood and the walnut, that is formed like a brain, could be a remedy for the brains.

Nowadays many people laugh about these unscientific conclusions, see them as naive or simple magical thinking.

But this believing is not so naive, as the believe, a laughing AI robot or a robot speaking friendly words, that this robot is feeling happy or friendly. If one does not know much about the reactions of a human body, it is not the most silly thing, to think, that similarities in form or color might indicate a medical effect onto similar human physical structures. There is even a (small) probability that the similarity has a common reason. It could have been - as long as it is not chemical tested - that a red thing has elements within, which help to build the red blood (it could be iron), or that a walnut, looking like a little brain, has for some common reason the same outside structure as the human brain. And for that reason it was presumed in old times, that perhaps it could help as a medicine at brain diseases.

But from a robot with AI we know, why it is smiling like a

human, or why it is asking in a friendly way: "How was your day today?". We know, that humans programmed the robot to do that, and that it is also perhaps programmed to learn by itself in observing, in which situations smiling or friendly words might be a desired or useful gesture. A robot with AI could learn about human behavior by itself, it could learn the outer forms of behavior by seeing many many videos with interacting humans. But to believe, that along with this programming and learning there are real emotions arising within the robot, is more naive, than the believe in the "Signaturenlehre". It is deeper a magical belief, than most people might realize.

The smile on the face of a robot with AI is determined by calculated movements of beforehand constructed mechanics. The apparatus is constructed by humans, who want the robots to be successful, to make people admire the engineers work and later on to buy the robots or give more money for research. The nice words of a robot are a mechanism, for that technical constructions like an apparatus imitating human voices, were installed. And learning was done. The AI robot had to learn, at what situations to use certain words would be successful in view of the aim the IT programmer has in mind. And the AI robot had learned, in which way gestures or words are connected with the outer world. And the robot now uses Artificial Intelligence to use gestures and words in a way that they might fulfill the programmed aims (which could mean to manipulate humans). But the robot is not using his "knowledge" to make the robot´s heart happy (it has no heart). Happiness does mean nothing to the AI robot.

The smiling does not imply, that the robot, even with all his Artificial Intelligence and all his learning, has feelings. Intelligence is not necessarily connected with emotions, it can be pure calculating - and in the robot, it is pure calculating, it is cold Artificial Intelligence.

There are no hormones, no neurotransmitters and messenger substances are secreted, no brain areal is firing out of joy, no inner reactions of joy can be found (as heart acceleration or glinting eyes or changing of the breathing, better digestion and the many healthy effects, that joy may have). And these are only physical reactions, that are connected with emotions - but even they are missing. The feelings themselves are not there at all. At least we have no true reason to believe, that there are emotions in a robot.

But almost everyone is having some feelings himself or herself, when seeing and observing a humanoid robot with Artificial Intelligence like Sophia (there is a lot and astounding material about the humanoid robot Sophia to be found in YouTube). We cannot other, than reacting to some degree emotional, when a robot is outward constructed so human-like. And Sophia, together with other high developed AI robots, to some degree shows a behavior that is well known for us humans and is appreciated.

Everyone knows, that inside a screen, that is showing a video, there are no real people living. And the robot with AI is not having the feelings it seems to demonstrate. The screen is only a chemical construction, on which lights pop up in different colors, so that we can see a picture. But the picture turns into real persons in our head, but not in the screen. And so a robot, that imitates the gestures of a friendly person and imitates the way of speaking, that it has learned from observing friendly persons, is in no way feeling friendly at that moment. It is only calculating.

With the screen, it is not difficult for us humans to understand, that the screen is not containing the persons itself. But with a well build AI robot, that is very well imitating the look and behavior of humans, it is much more difficult to remain distant and see only the technique behind.

And most of us do not even understand the more simple technique, for example, how the transmitting of data from one smart phone to another smart phone is working. But we understand, that the face that is speaking on the screen, is the face of our friend on the other side of the line speaking also into a smart phone. But that is a real person at the other end. Different it is already with games, there the figures are constructed, even the abilities they have in movement and decision are programmed. There might be a real other person playing its avatar, or the figure is total guided by the programming. These things make a mixed reality.

But we still know, the person on the screen is not here, it is only a game or a picture and the real person could be far away. The screen is much too flat, there could be no real human inside it. But this is other when we meet humanoid robots that have the shape of a human, the way of moving like a human and gestures like a human. And with Artificial Intelligence they seem to behave and speak like a human. Here our instinct gets very much deceived.

A robot with AI is so complex, that perhaps only the constructing engineer might understand it - and perhaps not even he at full. When the AI robot is learning by itself, the engineer might not any more know all that is happening inside the calculating programs of the robot. But when it is a human-like looking and a human-like behaving robot, it is much easier to think, we can understand this robot. We seem to understand it easier, than we do, when we think about the function of a smart phone or the GPS. So the absurd situation is, that we instinctively think to understand an apparatus, that is one of the technical most advanced ones, and most difficult and complex to understand. The human appearance and the human way of acting can fascinate us so much, that we do not think any more about the complex technique behind the words, gestures and movements, a technique most of us do not understand at all. Our instinct tells us: yes, we understand what we see and what the AI robot is thinking and feeling. It almost certainly will touch our heart, if the humanoid robot is smiling and speaking friendly words. We would be no normal humans, if we would not react on such a smile.

Are we perhaps so much conditioned in our understanding of human behavior over thousands of evolutionary years, that we have no chance to see a smiling robot in a pure technical way? Will a smiling face always touch our heart? Or other imitated human gestures? What will that mean for our future together with human looking AI robots?

Is energy 4-dimensional, because it needs time for making a change? Is light close to the mind?

Some aspects of the energy lead to the idea, that energy might be 4-dimensional (maybe in mathematics and astrophysics there are already many thoughts about dimensions and energy existing, I admit, that I am not informed well enough to know this).

Energy has no normal physical 3-dimensional body.

Energy is that, what can cause changes. And changes need time. So there cannot be any effect of energy without the dimension of time.

Energy has no body, it can alter its manifestation, it can be a wave, it can be gravitation, it can be movement, it can be heat, it can be a chemical bond, it can be power of deformation, it can be electrical, magnetic and so on. But what always remains is the same power of changing. The same energy amount - in whatever form it appears, has always the same power to change something.

Changing something is in other words the ability to reach into the future, to reach into a time-space.

So perhaps energy itself is 4-dimensional or at least near to the 4-dimensional world, perhaps it is the cause for a 4-dimensional world to exist.

Or it is the power to expand into time, perhaps it is the time itself.

Perhaps it is not accidentally, that in old times mind and light were seen quite close. The physicist Arthur Zajonc has written a book 1993 with the title "The Entwined History of Light and Mind" - a very interesting book, describing how in old times light and mind were seen together, then came a time where they were looked on totally isolated, and after that, with the quantum physics they were seen again in relationship to each other.

I am not a physicist, but I see, that the light is in some aspects as mysterious to the physicists as it is the mind to all of us. Maybe that has to some part to do with the 4-dimensional world, that also eludes a complete understanding of science.

Feeling - connected with 4-dimensional imagination and with remembering

Emotions and feelings are very close connected with imagination. Emotions and feelings are much more than only a "yes-no", a black-and white judgment that is combined with many "when" and "if". Emotions judge as well, they tell us, how something does feel, but in a much deeper and rounder way than the cold and point-sharp "it works" or "it does not work". It is with the over-viewing looking at a time-space, with that emotions and feelings arise.

A fresh fallen in love person at work is looking forward towards a date in the evening and is getting happy and excited by imagining the evening.

A person, who has lost someone very dear to him, will get sad by remembering nice times with that person.

In both cases the feelings are in a double sense connected with imagination and time-space. Both feelings arise when the person is looking into another time-space than that the person is in at the moment. And people can be joyful looking forward on emotions that they expect feeling in the future or they can be remembering the emotions they have felt in a past time.

A more simple feeling of longing can arise by a chair: the

longing to sit down. It arises, if someone is very tired because of having been a long time walking or standing or because of being very weak. Someone in a very tired condition
will remember how relaxing and pleasant it will be to sit
down. But he will not remember one single isolated moment
of sitting, not just the beginning time-point-moment or a
middle moment of sitting, or the moment, when he will rise
again - he will imagine a longer time-space in which the
muscles slowly relax and recover. He will imagine the
process of changing from tired legs towards again powerful
legs.

The chair will not always rise this feeling of longing. It also
can rise anger: if the chair in a small flat is standing in the
pathway, it can hinder quick moving. A person might imagine walking quick from one part of the flat to another and is
hindered by the chair - the imagination of coming quickly to
the other spot is crossed by the chair. Now the image
changes and the person thinks, how difficult it is to walk
through the flat, and he gets angry and kicks away the chair
with his foot, with imagining, that on the way back he can
pass more easily.

Emotions can be mixed with different feelings. So I can feel
happy, because I am on my way to a beach that I will visit
on my holiday. But at the same time I can be nervous and
anxious, because on the way to the airport I got into a traffic
jam and in my mind there is the fear that I might miss my
plane. But again, at the same time, I feel a bit relieved, because my little daughter, sitting beside me in the car, got

asleep and so is not getting fretful and nervous, as I feared before.

I don´t know, if there is a way existing, where emotions and feelings can arise without looking into a time-space. Can they arise from one instant, without combining this instant with past or future situations and changing?

Perhaps it happens, when I cut my finger with a knife. But also then the pain is influenced by the situation. If I am doing something very important and I am in a great hurry, I will not pay so much attention to the cut as when I am having much time and no special aim in mind. Or Christian martyrs in earlier history were sometimes suffering great pains with a smile on their face, expecting soon to be in heaven.

Someone going through physical or psychological pain can sustain this pain better and longer, if he or she has an imagination of a very positive aim, and the pains are only seen as necessary for reaching the aim. Soldiers going willingly into war are an example (even if this example sounds a bit strange today, where at least in Europe the last wars are decades away), but also a fire-fighter rescuing a little child is an example, or a politician going through harsh critics because at the end he thinks he will achieve a positive aim, or a mother that is accepting patiently the troubles of a pregnancy while she is happily looking forward to the birth of the child.

I cannot imagine the arising of hope or fear, joy or sadness or other emotions without any accompanying imagination of some sort of development and changing.

The word "feeling" is spoken in a long stretched way - as if in this way it is already indicated, that feelings reach often far into the future or the past.

How complicated the arising of emotions and feelings may be - they are always connected with imaginations and influenced by expectations one has in mind. So they reach into the time-space. And together with the mind, feelings and emotions arise on a 4-dimensional background.

Will robots with AI be able to have emotions? And where could be found an emotion-particle, perhaps in electricity?

Can a robot, calculating with 1-dimensional numbers, that means with data that are reduced to numbers - can a robot have emotions and feelings?

The first problem is, that the information is 1-dimensional given to the robot. But the other second problem comes because a robot is constructed physically in a 3-dimensional world.

Perhaps there is a 4-dimensional aspect in the robot, because it is using energy. The robot uses energy not only for moving, but also to run its calculations. Energy might perhaps be the 4th dimension within the robot.

But the 4-dimensional aspect seems not to be complex within a computer. It is reduced to "Yes" - electric current flowing and "No" - current not flowing. There are conditions, when it is flowing and when it is not flowing. These conditions are one-dimensional complex (I myself do not know the exact construction of a computer). But as far as I can understand it, this complexity is predestined within the hardware, within the physical 3-dimensional construction of the computer or the robot and programmed onto a 3-dimensional hard disk. The pure energy - as a current - is flowing or not flowing. But energy can much more than only flowing or not flowing like it is the case with the current in the computer: energy can change its effect, energy can be given further on to something else, energy can be changing the form and character (for example: heat can start a chemical reaction, then the energy of the heat can be saved within a chemical molecule, light shining onto leaves can be altered into the energy that is being stored in the sugar-molecule).

So I cannot see, how complex 4-dimensional feelings and emotions should come just from a current flowing or not flowing. By its influence on the 3-dimensional physical world a current can direct an apparatus, that is constructed to react on small electrical impulses in a physical way - but this has nothing to do with emotions. Perhaps the current is "happy" if it can flow. But is there a deeper feeling, a complicated feeling? I doubt it.

Up to now, I have not heard of any feeling-particle that was found. Up till now only the information leading towards feelings is observed. But information is not the same as feeling. If it would be so, a television showing a sad situation would be sad. Or the word "happiness" would itself be happy. To evoke feelings and emotions, for that the information has to be read by an organism that is capable of feelings and emotions.

Information can be calculated, can regulate processes, can be combined with other information - but it is always only telling "Yes" or "No", possible or not possible, current can flow or not. Much is possible with this quantity-calculating programs, and they can influence the 3-dimensional physical world, because the computer or robot has a 3-dimensional hardware, that can regulate the world outside. So a robot can do work.

And a robot by now can smile - but it is only an outer form of the 3-dimensional expression of joy, but it is not regulated by joy, it is regulated by calculation. So it is with friendly words of an AI robot, when it is asking the human, how he feels, how it was in work, what he wants to eat and so on. These are calculated terms, because by observation (winning data of probability and using this data) the robot learned what words cause a positive answering reaction from the human - and what is to be seen as a positive reaction: most likely this has been programmed by a human.

There might one day be robots, which learn without any aim given by a human software engineer - but that they are learning at all, this has to be programmed one time from outside as an aim - if done so, the learning might run by itself.

But nevertheless there are no true deeper emotions involved. The robot is just doing, what on the basic of flowing or hindered current is to do. A robot will destroy himself without any emotion, if it is coming to the conclusion, that this is what the calculating of its data tells. It might even go by itself to a recycling place, so that its parts might be used for a new robot or something else.

The particle, that is evoking emotions and feelings is not yet found. To me it seems, that science is not even looking to find one. Perhaps there is the believe, that the reception (with eye, ear, nerves endings) of data, transmitted towards the brain and combined with other data might be enough to build up emotions and feelings.

But is it like this? Where in that abstract world is the feeling? Inside an atom, inside an electron, inside a ray of light? What do we really know about the place of the emotion and how it arises or subsides? I think, in this respect we are still very ignorant.

It is rather easy, to tell what a nerve is, what an impulse is, what an electron in the 3-dimensional physical world is, and what effect it has on the surrounding. It has an effect, that can be repeated again and again.

But in the realm of emotions and feelings the exact measuring becomes difficult. Already the defining of an exact emotion is difficult. Sadness or joy, happiness or fear - they have so many different faces. And how can I describe an emotion exactly? I only can register, what a person is saying or doing, who says, at this moment he or she has a special emotion. But is the emotion correctly described? There is also the possibility to observe cerebric activities in the brain. But is the activity the emotion itself? Has then the current in our electrical current lines emotions as well? Where does an emotion sit? In what 3-dimensional physics, in electricity or other forms of energy? Is emotion 4-dimensional and can because of that not be found in a 3-dimensional world?

Perhaps this inability to say something physical concrete about emotions has to do with the mind, and with the 4-dimensional holistic view of the mind.

The togetherness of calculating, mind and feeling

If the hypothesis is right that the mind and the feeling are ex-isting in a 4-dimensional way, then nevertheless the mind also has to do with the 2- and the 3-dimensional physical world and with the 1-dimensional calculating world, and with the world of "Yes" and "No".

Our mind can realize: something is working or is not: "Yes-No"-dimension (Zero-dimension?).
Our mind can count and calculate - the 1-dimensional world.
Our mind realizes surfaces like the ground level of our earth with hills and valleys - the 2-dimensional world (if you only look onto the surface, not onto the volume).
Our mind is working with a 3-dimensional physical "hard-ware", with our nerves and ganglions.
And our mind can imagine the future and remember the past: the 4-dimensional world.

So our mind is capable to wander in all 4 dimensions and to combine them.

We can, for example, calculate, how much money we will need in holiday and we can decide: yes, we can do it, or no, it is too expensive. We can see, how the country in our holi-day area is build with the surface, if it has steep hills or if it is flat, we can find the place on a map, we can travel with a real 3-dimensional car or train or plane to the holiday place, our body then arrives in its 3-dimensional physical form at that place. And we can imagine how the holidays will be, or we can remember, how they were.

All the dimensions form a picture and make it possible for us to shape our life within the possibilities our surrounding is offering us. We are able to realize possibilities and to do things to make them come true. It is amazing, if one looks closer, what our mind is able to do in every moment, in great events and in everyday habits. Our mind (and also that of animals) has the fascinating ability to combine different worlds of different number of dimensions.

Will robots feel emotions like humans? And what, if not so?

Will robots one day feel emotions like humans? I don´t believe so.

But what is, if they are not having feelings like humans?

There are two imaginable scenarios:

The robots will never have deeper feelings (perhaps some relief if the current is allowed to flow, but perhaps not even that). Then they will never have an individual "I", an individual own personality wanting things. They learn what to want by exact calculation or also by trying randomly. They have one programmed last aim that is tried to reach with all learning and calculating. This aim is either programmed by an human, or by another computer, but at the end somewhere there was a human, starting it all. Or the aim is totally randomly, but I do not think that it will happen that robots come into being just by coincidence - but who knows.

But in all these robots there is no controlling by deeper feelings. They can be programmed to every possible aim - useful or not - it only depends on the programmer. And it is the question, what by learning by themselves, they would do to reach the aim. Will they help humans and living beings, or will they suddenly find it better to destroy life? And by a mistake, can there change aims, from the good (for us humans) to the bad?

The other scenario would be: robots learn to feel emotions. But as we have up to now no real idea, what - from a scientific and engineering point of view - feelings and emotions are, and where they are placed, so it would be quite "spooky" if we suddenly realize that AI robots have feelings of their own. Or IT-programmers find at least really a primitive way to install emotions within a robot. But how would they work? We do not understand fully our own emotions, and a lot of harm and confusion comes by our emotions (perhaps this is necessary, do we know that?) - could we be sure, that emotional robots with Artificial Intelligence will not be disastrous?

Emotions can be much stronger than logical reasoning - do we want robots to be lead by emotions?

Over-viewing events, embedded in great time-spaces - is this 5-dimensional - when time itself gets not only a point or a line but a volume?

A higher dimension is over-viewing a lower one, and the lower dimension is limiting the higher one.

We are capable to overview not only one event in full length from beginning to the end one moment after the other. We can look at it and see backwards and forwards - such as an novel-author can write first the beginning and the end of a novel and after that may be starting to write the part in the middle (or we can read the novel not only from beginning to end, instead we could pick up the chapters we like most).

And we can not look only on one event, we can look on more events together and combine them to a more composited event. A good example is the football or soccer match. The football players have to conceive the actions (events) of their own team and also of the rival team. A player has to try to foresee the combined actions of all others on the field and then to plan his own action. Or a manager has to overview all the work his employees are doing, so he can coordinate the total work in a useful way. He not only has to calculate facts and pure data, but he also has to consider the emotions and characters of his employees. He will form a holistic picture of the situation. Or a mother has to have many things in mind together, when she is handling, educating, animating, controlling their children and caring for them. She has in mind a holistic picture, what kind of person her child is, and from that she decides what might be good for the child.

So our mind is not like a film camera, unwinding the scenes of a story, it is much more, the mind is realizing events as a whole, seeing them in the context of many other events, and, that is most important: the mind is judging events logically but also emotionally.

Our mind accompanies every realization, every thought, every plan, every imagination or every memory with feelings connected with aims. The feelings might be very subtle or very unimportant and almost not felt consciously, or they might be loud and dominating. But in any case they are there, connected with what the mind realizes or imagines.

Is it not so, that at the end, all our aims, all what we desire, what we long for, what we appreciate, all that at the end has its source in emotions? Do we not want, to feel good, and not to feel bad in the end? The way to reach good feeling might be very different - but wanting to feel basically (not only for a short moment) well, is that longing not the power that makes us do things, that urges us to go through our life and to fulfill what seems important for us? And do we not feel happy, if we come nearer to our aim, and depressed, if we see, that we cannot reach it?

Are it not the emotions, that let us feel a meaning of life? Is logic regulating our emotions, or are our emotions using logic, to reach the aims that are deep inside our soul?

But if we need to overview many events, and to look in the past and into the future, to find our personal way, to understand, what is important for us, to find in the end the meaning of our life - is it then not possible, that the meaning of life is an even higher dimension than the 4th dimension. Could it be, that the meaning of life is felt with a sense, that is connected with a 5th or even higher dimension?

From a higher dimension the lower ones can be overviewed. From the feeling of the meaning of life, we can judge what is good for us and what is unhealthy for our soul.

Often from the lower dimensions, from the events in and around us, we get hindered to do, what we would like to do. Is that the limitation of the lower dimension? Is this on one side, what makes us to individuals, being different from others, but is it also that, what is limiting us? Is it the prize to be an individual, to lose the sensation of being always in a holistic way in one with the meaning of the world? And are we living our lives trying to unify our individual life again with the holistic meaning of being? Are there higher dimensions than the well known four dimensions - dimensions that are not physically or mathematically calculated, but felt within us, when we feel alive?

Life and feelings - are they not still like a wonder for us?

Epilogue

If it is true, that the mind together with feelings and emotions reaches into 4 dimensions (by remembering and imagining), then it is never possible for a 3-dimensional body that is working with 1-dimensional data, that it will be the same as a human being. And a robot, even an AI robot, will never really become like humans.

The fundamental question to this is: is our mind creating memories and imagination also only by calculating certain points? Is the mind taking certain points out of the full time, like a computer does, or does the mind "walk around" in the time with a holistic view? Are events in memories and in imagination pictures of many single "pixels", or are they something continuous - even if in remembering and in imagination some situations are clearer and deeper than others.

As our 3-dimensional physical world of bodies and objects is not the same as a calculated "pixel-picture" of our world and its objects, so it can very well be true, that our imagination and our memories are not the same as the 3-dimensional physical world. It can very well be, that they reach into the time in a real 4-dimensional way. Our 3-dimensional body cannot follow, because it lives for our realization only in a "now-point-moment" and cannot leave it.

But our mind together with feelings can wander freely in the time-space.

The 1-dimensional world of numbers and combining them in calculation is something else than the 3-dimensional physical world of bodies and both are something else than our 4 dimensional mind. They are not separated in a way, that one dimension has nothing to do with the other, but the higher dimensions are getting structure by the lower ones, and the lower ones are over-viewed and its elements seen together and in their positions to one another (like elements in a picture) from the view of the higher dimension.

Astrophysics talks nowadays sometimes about much more dimensions, but these dimensions are used in calculations, to find a way to calculate the whole world with all sorts of energies. But as far as I know, they don´t see an special element of our mind in it.

But it may be, that there are even more dimensions in another way, and that the meaning of our life comes from the glance into a higher dimension, a dimension over-viewing our whole life and the being of everything. Who knows.

At the end I do not want to be analyzing, but I will describe a picture, a scene (closing the circle to Paul McCartney´s "Fool on the Hill"). Will one day robots feel like Mark and Rose on a hill like in the following scene?

Mark and Rose had climbed a high mountain. Now they reached the summit - and a grand view is opening to them.

In one direction ridge after ridge of mountains is rising, till far away they are getting blue and dim in the haze. In the other direction the mountain is sloping down, and Mark and Rose can look down onto low hills, and further behind the land stretches out as a great plain. A sparkling river is meandering between green meadows and darker woodlands, bringing towards the ocean since unknown ages the water coming down by rainfalls. Birds are circling around in the blue sky. Somewhere in the distance clouds are forming and disappearing again. The air is fresh and clear.

Slowly the sun is setting, evening is coming, birds are singing their evening song. The shadows get longer, the valleys are already quite dark. The colors change into variations of gray, and then begin to turn into black. The sky becomes deep dark blue, the evening star is rising. Somewhere a dog is barking. The bells of a distant church are ringing for the evening prayer, telling about the people having since numberless generations a confidence, that within our world there is a good spirit to rely on - in good times and in bad times. And in old times they used to pray to this good spirit before nightfall, and some people still do.

And now the night is rising, with a deep and wide black - but not without far lights. A small waxing moon is to be seen, and more and more stars begin to shine, and the more dark the night is becoming the more bright they glint. In the deep dark the sky is spangled with stars, the Milky Way shows its glittering band over the width of the whole sky, telling of numerous other worlds out there, some very old and some arising newly within millions of aeons. This vastness of the universe Mark and Rose can only look at wondering.

After standing for a while looking in the sky full of stars, Mark and Rose walk to the little hut nearby, taking there a simple evening meal and then going to sleep, confident that the next morning the sun will rise again, and a new day will begin.

124   For reader's notes